REV. DR. KEVIN W. COSBY

GET OFF YOUR BUT!

MESSAGES, MUSINGS, AND MINISTRIES TO EMPOWER THE AFRICAN AMERICAN CHURCH

GET OFF YOUR BUT!

Messages, Musings, and Ministries
to Empower the African American Church

Get Off Your But!

Kevin W. Cosby

Copyright © 2000

Revised 2014, 2017

© 2017, Revised Edition

Paperback Edition: ISBN: 978-0-9785572-4-9

Kindle (mobi) Edition: ISBN 978-0-9785572-5-6

Epub Edition: ISBN 978-0-9785572-6-3

Printed in the United States of America

10 9 8 7 6 5 4 3

SIMMONS
P R E S S

Louisville, Kentucky

— TABLE OF CONTENTS —

— DEDICATION —

This book is dedicated to my late parents, Laken Cosby, Jr., and Cora Elizabeth Miller Cosby, who gave me the gift of physical and spiritual life, and who encouraged me to always make the most of that life.

. . . . . .

To my pastors, my grandfather, the late Reverend Dr. B.J. Miller, Sr., whose deep devotion first inspired me. To the late Reverend Dr. Charles Mims, Jr., whose encouraging words have lifted me. And also to the Reverend Dr. A.C. Goodloe, whose practical wisdom has guided me.

. . . . . .

To my stepmother, Connie Wade Cosby, whose love inspired in me the desire to grow both mentally and intellectually.

. . . . . .

To the members of St. Stephen Baptist Church, who have grown with me over the years and have made me proud to be your pastor.

. . . . . .

To my children, Christine Nicole and Kevin Christopher, who have always made me feel proud and privileged to be the man you call, "Dad."

. . . . . .

To my wife, Barnetta Turner Cosby, my best friend and the wind beneath my wings. God continues to speak to me through you.

— ACKNOWLEDGMENT —

I wish to acknowledge
the editorial assistance of
the Reverend Olivia M. Cloud, who aided me
in bringing *Get Off Your But!* to completion.

— FOREWORD —

Sermons are not the most popular form of reading. It is difficult to encourage listening to sermons; it is far more difficult to encourage through reading a deeper intellectual encounter. For most, sermons are a rather dull and laborious exercise in unraveling the obvious in worn and ancient texts. Often sermons are designed to make us feel good—a weekly spiritual "high"— without challenging us to be or become our better selves.

In *Get Off Your But!* Kevin Cosby transcends sermonic stereotypes and offers a new paradigm for the proclamation of the Gospel. Through these pages you will find engaging sermons that are laced with sparkling intellectual thought and solid biblical exegesis. A great value of this writing is to be found in the "Musings," which immediately follow each sermon and which require of the reader a more profound engagement with the written sermonic word and the contemporary meanings of the biblical text.

Of even greater importance is his insistence on ministry that flows from the message. Here you will find clear and definitive ways for the preached word to become operative and significant in the life of the local congregation. The "Ministries" section of this writing is literally capable of transforming churches in terms of their programmatic design. Use these thoughtful suggestions and your church will never be the same!

These are not sermons for the sake of writing sermons. They are sermons with purpose and intent to serve and edify the ministry and the church. Dr. Cosby's anointment leaps from the pages with astounding impact on the reader.

This is a prophetic writing. It stands within that tradition that speaks on behalf of God a word that most of us did not want to hear. It is a challenging word that moves us beyond complacency and mediocrity and will not let us preach or manage the ministry of the church with a "business as usual" attitude.

Kevin Cosby helps us to see ourselves in the man at the contemporary Bethesda Pool and Spa. He does not ignore contemporary pain, but he will not permit us to blame others for our brokenness. He challenges us to healthy, nutritional eating habits. He points us to Sabbath rest and dares us to avoid what has been termed the Messiah Complex. He insists that our churches must be multi-dimensional and offers practical suggestions for the creation of faith-based community development corporations. When Dr. Cosby opens the African window, a fresh breeze of relevance blows into the church. Here the writer reminds us of our African heritage, the importance of our African culture, and the responsibility we have to answer Countee Cullen's question: "What is Africa to me?" With bold and dramatic strokes this preacher reminds us of the value of affirming who we are in order that the people who fill our pews are both enlightened and empowered, like Daniel, to escape the den of exploitation, dislocation and marginalization. These are not timid offerings.

The tragedy of this writing is that we do not hear Kevin Cosby preach these powerful words. This young Joshua is, without question, an anointed man of God. He is a sensitive person, an authentic pastor and an articulate spokesman for the living Christ. He is scholarly without being boring. The lessons contained in this volume are the foundation stones upon which he has built one of the most creative, socially sensitive and biblically based congregations in America. He has captured the minds and the hearts of his people, and in so doing, he has honored our Christ and done great service to the St. Stephen's church.

This is a book worth reading. When you read this book, your life will be better, your community will be stronger, and your church will be more relevant. But first, you must get off your but!

Rev. H. Beecher Hicks, D. Min.
Metropolitan Baptist Church
Washington, D.C.

— INTRODUCTION —

It has been noted that the Gospel has a dual responsibility: "afflicting the comfortable and comforting the afflicted." Afflicting the comfortable occurs when Christ disrupts our world and shakes us from our tranquil complacency, self-contentment and self-satisfaction. Comforting the afflicted happens when Christ gives assurance, solace and strength to the world's hurting in order to help them move forward toward wholeness.

Historically, the African American Church, through both protest and advocacy, has afflicted the comfortable. The voices of our forebears such as Richard Allen, Harriet Tubman, Ida B. Wells, Martin Luther King Jr. and others, have always spoken out against oppressive systems. The Church must diligently and faithfully continue this mission and tradition of sowing seeds of affliction in a world made comfortable by self-centeredness and self-indulgence.

The seeds of affliction we sow in the name of Jesus must have purpose and redemptive value. The Gospels cite many instances of Jesus afflicting the comfortable. Our Lord did not have disagreements with others because He was in a bad mood and wanted to take it out on others. His many clashes with the religious leadership of His day occurred because He boldly dared to make them aware of their own moral failings in the sight of God. His confrontations with them held them into account concerning their faith and devotion to God.

The Church must work with equal diligence, however, to carry out the mandate of the Gospel in comforting the afflicted. The Gospel message does not simply offer words of comfort. The Gospel is comfort. To withhold that message from those who need to hear it is akin to withholding water from one who is dying of thirst.

The Gospel gives many instances of Jesus comforting the afflicted. Crowds followed Him because they knew He had the power

1

to heal the sick, raise the dead, comfort the grief-stricken and feed the hungry. Jesus brought solace to the multitudes because of His powers to heal and comfort. Through Him, all believers can offer healing and comfort to those who are suffering without.

But we must be prudent in our ministries to provide aid and comfort. Some of those who sought Jesus' help were like the man at the Pool of Bethesda. At the pool were those whom the King James Version describes as "impotent folk." They were people unable to function as they ought. They were lame and incompetent regarding their designed purpose. The man Jesus approached claimed to want help, but he was unwilling to offer any more than excuses to move himself closer to healing. The man perceived himself to be a victim, dependent on the compassion of another to lift him into the pool. Jesus told the man to pick up his own bed and walk (John 5:8). The comfort we offer in the name of Jesus must move beyond dependency and victimology toward self-empowerment and wholeness.

"Get off your but!" is a message that, in some area of life, every person needs to hear. Every person can look at an area and recognize a need to get off a "but" that is holding him or her back. We all know at least one person who constantly offers excuses for not tackling some difficulty in life. The challenge is different for every human being. The list is as old as humanity itself: substance abuse, unemployment, poverty, overeating, gossip, sexual promiscuity and marital infidelity, explosive temper, jealously, sloth, covetousness, fear, and the list goes on. We allow these things to hold us back, with only a "but" standing between us and wholeness. The paralytic offered Jesus a "but" that day at the pool of Bethesda to explain his condition.

We all know that some circumstances cannot be changed. What can always be changed, however, is our attitude toward those circumstances. Consider the life of W. Mitchell. At the age of 46, he was burned beyond recognition in a motorcycle accident. Four years after his accident, Mitchell was piloting a plane that crashed and rendered him paralyzed from the waist down. By this time, Mitchell explained, "I was wondering what the hell was happening to me!" His two accidents left his face a patchwork quilt of color as a result of multiple skin grafts. The motorcycle accident left him without fingers or toes. The plane crash left his legs immobile.

Temporarily set back but undaunted by his misfortunes, Mitchell became a millionaire, a sought-after public speaker, a happy newlywed, and mayor of Crest Butte, Colorado. He later campaigned for a Congressional seat. He used his disfigured appearance as an asset with campaign slogans like, "Not just another pretty face."

Most of us will never know the kind of affliction that Mitchell endured. Few people could demonstrate his resilience in the face of tragedy. Mitchell offered no "buts" to excuse an unproductive life. "I am in charge of my own spaceship," he has said. "I could choose to see this situation as a setback or a starting point." He and a couple of friends started a wood burning stove company that became the second largest employer in the state of Vermont.

— CHAPTER ONE —

Get Off Your But!

And a certain man was there, which had an infirmity thirty and eight years. When Jesus saw him lie, and knew that he had been now a long time in that case, he saith unto him, Wilt thou be made whole? (John 5:5-6, KJV)

The city of Jerusalem was abuzz with activity. Pious pilgrims from Palestine and the Jewish Diaspora had flooded the beloved City of David to participate in a sacred religious festival. Among the crowd of pilgrims was Jesus and His disciples, singing along with the joyous crowds, "I was glad when they said unto me let us go into the house of the Lord, Our feet shall stand within thy gates, O Jerusalem" (Psalm 122:1-2).

In the midst of this conviviality, Jesus slipped away and headed toward a place called the pool of Bethesda. He left the celebrating crowds to go to suffering humanity. The pool of Bethesda was a sort of outdoor intensive-care unit. The clientele who hovered in and around the pool consisted of those who were blind, lame, paralyzed, wounded and broken—both physically and spiritually. Upon nearing the pool of Bethesda, one was accosted by the odors associated with illness and unkempt bodies, co-mingled with the agonizing sounds of excruciating pain and their associated feelings of isolation and desperation suspended in the air.

Waiting all around the pool of Bethesda lay a depressingly pitiful company of sick and dying people whose only hope lay in the merciful moving of the water. Superstition held that an angel would come down and trouble the water and whoever was first in the pool, would be healed of his or her infirmity. This story is the basis for the slave song, "Wade in the Water:"

Wade in the water,
Wade in the water children,
Wade in the water,
God gonna' trouble the water.

Churches today still sing this song at baptism, but the song originally served as instructions to runaway slaves. The message to the runaways was that they should wade in the water so that the blood hounds could not pick up their scent because God troubled the water.

So at the pool of Bethesda, an assembly of the infirmed were putting their hope in bubbles. They attributed the bubbling action in the water to the work of angels commissioned to God's special healing ministry. It is true that those who waded in the water experienced something medicinal; however, it was not due to angelic agitation. The spade of the archaeologist has since ascribed the bubbling of the water to a subterranean stream that periodically made the bubbles surface to the top.

Around the pool of Bethesda lay a company of sick and dying people waiting for the medicinal movement of the water to occur. On this particular Sabbath, Jesus bypassed the Temple filled with religious folk and went to the pool where suffering humanity lay. Today, His actions would be equivalent to a prominent preacher attending a national religious convention and instead of proceeding to the convention hall, showing up at the emergency room of the largest indigent care hospital of that city. While such an action is totally out of character for delegates to a religious conference, it is totally within the realm of goodness, holiness, mercy, kindness and self-giving that is characteristic of our Savior.

Among the company of the sick and dying at the pool of Bethesda was a paralytic who had infirmed for thirty-eight years and had been waiting diligently by the pool for quite some time. When Jesus saw the man lying there, He asked him a question that has puzzled Bible expositors throughout Christian history. Jesus asked, "Wilt thou be made whole?"

At first glance, Jesus' question may seem foolish or, at best, insensitive. This man had been suffering from an illness that had rendered him paralyzed for thirty-eight long years. He essentially had been totally incapacitated for his entire adult life. Thirty-eight years is a long time to be flat on your back. Jesus found him by the pool of Bethesda searching for a miracle and, instead of feeling sorry for him, Jesus asked, "Do you want to be healed?"

What kind of question is that to ask a sick, suffering human being? It is like asking a drowning woman who is about to go under, "Do you want to be rescued?" It is like a surgeon in the operating room asking a patient, "Do you want me to perform the operation that you need to save your life?" It is like a paramedic asking a man who has been shot, "Do you want to go to the hospital?"

All of these questions may seem superfluous, but Jesus' question went beyond the surface to address the root cause of the man's sickness. In no other instance do the Gospels record that Jesus asked such a question to a hurting person. When a leper came to Him is search of healing, Jesus did not ask him, "Do you want healing?" In the case of this paralytic, however, Jesus was moved to ask, "Do you want to be healed?"

Jesus discerned that this man was more neurotic than paralytic. He recognized not only the symptom of his illness—paralysis—but the cause of his illness that was rooted in both mental and emotional issues.

Centuries before the emergence of modern psychology, Jesus recognized that human beings are psychophysical organisms. Many physical ailments are sometimes psychologically and mentally induced. We human beings often act, feel and perform according to our mental blueprint. If a person is convinced that he or she is at the North Pole, that person will begin to feel cold. The nervous system cannot tell the difference between an imagined experience and a real one. While this man's illness was real, the source of his illness was more mental than physical.

I am not espousing any form of mind science, such as Christian Scientists, New Ageism or Hinduism. These schools of thought espouse the notion that all diseases are illusions, unrealities, or what the Hindus call Maya—conditions that can be banished with positive thinking. There is also the school of "quick fix" evangelists who tell people that "true" believers don't get sick if they hold certain thoughts in their minds. All rational Christians know that pain and suffering are real experiences.

An amusing anecdote illustrates my point: A boxer was being pulverized by his opponent. To inspire confidence in the badly beaten fighter, his manager told him between rounds: "He never laid a glove on you." Exasperated, the boxer finally quipped: "If he never laid a glove on me, somebody needs to watch the referee because somebody is beating the hell out of me!"

African Americans know that pain and suffering are real. Our people have developed an entire genre of music to articulate our pain experience—the blues.

> *My man left this morning, just about half past four.*
> *He left a note on the pillow saying he can't use me no more.*
>
> *It was hard to take, it was such a bitter pill, if the blues don't kill me then that man's meanness will.*
>
> *I was born in the country, I was raised on a ghetto street. Ever since I was old enough to be one, I've been a victim of every woman I meet.*
>
> *Every time I meet a pretty girl, I lose my self-control. It's bad to lose your self-control, but every time you lose your bank roll.*
>
> *Country girls are slick, but city girls are slicker; but the way they keep slicking me, it keep getting me sicker and sicker and sicker.*

Pain is real. It is not an illusion. There are some sicknesses that are not in the mind, but are organic. There are times when you don't need a preacher, but a physician. There are some broken bodies that all the positive thinking in the world cannot pull back together. There are some amputated limbs that faith cannot restore. Believers in Jesus Christ are not required to make a choice between medicine versus prayer. Rather, we are to combine both medicine and prayer for effective healing.

Having established this necessity for physicians and others in the medical profession, the fact remains that some of our illnesses are mentally and psychologically conditioned. Jesus asked the paralyzed man, "Wilt thou be made whole?" Surely any person, if sufficiently motivated to be healed, could have found a way to get into the pool once in thirty-eight years! That's a lot of years. Thirty-eight years breaks down into 13,870 days. Before Jesus posed the question to him, the paralytic had missed 13,870 opportunities to get into the pool. That is why Jesus asked the man, "Do you want to be healthy?"

Implicit in the question is the hint the man was subconsciously evading help. In other words, Jesus was asking, "Are you ready to stop lying on that mat feeling sorry for yourself and expecting other people to feel sorry for you, too?" Some people who are sick could be well, but they are unwilling to let go of their illnesses. There are some people who are depressed and could recover, but they don't want to turn loose of their depression. There are some people who are promiscuous and could be under control, but they don't want to live manageable lives. There are some people who are trifling and could be respectable, productive human beings, but they find comfort in being trifling. Some people who are always having altercations are able to coexist more peacefully with others, but they thrive on creating conflict and dissension.

Jesus asked the man at the pool that day, as He is still asking all those who are hanging on to unnecessary pain and suffering, "Wilt thou be made whole?" The question is neither unnecessary nor insensitive. What would make any person want to hold on to an illness? The answer is simple, although it may be difficult to understand. An illness can become a way of life. It can become an easy way of manipulating others to gain attention, sympathy, resources or to dodge responsibility.

Sick people tend to be treated as victims. Many of them convince themselves and others that they can't help being the way they are. Shelby Steele, in his book, *The Content of Our Character* (Harper Perennial Library, 1991), states that all victims receive preferential treatment. He further asserts that every person in America is seeking to be a victim on some level because of a desire to gain preferential treatment. For example, African Americans are victims of slavery and racism. Jews are victims of the Holocaust and an anti-Semitic conspiracy. Women are victims of patriarchy and sexism. White men are now victims of reverse discrimination.

While it is true that atrocities committed against blacks during holocaust of slavery, the violation of Native Americans in the red holocaust, and the unspeakable horrors of the Jewish holocaust inflicted by the Nazis were real and produced unimaginable pain and suffering, it is also true that succeeding generations do not have to be perpetually victimized by these abominations. Victimization denies people the power to take control of their lives and keeps them under the control of their victimizers.

It is impossible to be both a producer and a victim. Victims are not expected to produce—e.g. work, pay restitution, or apologize for inappropriate behavior. They are not expected to take responsibility for their actions. Over the last seventy-five years our government has devised various programs to give temporary public assistance to people, including welfare, food stamps and subsidized housing, among other benefits. These provisions are often referred to as entitlement programs. The word *entitlement* means, "a title, right, or claim to something."

By referring to welfare as an entitlement, the impression is given that recipients are *entitled* to receive it and other forms of public assistance. As it was designed, public assistance in the form of welfare was meant to provide temporary or short-term aid to families. In that regard, every American is indeed entitled to receive assistance when in need, assuming the period of economic need would be temporary. The entitlement programs were never designed to be a long-term, multigenerational benefit. Yet welfare has produced perpetual victims of society, always needing some form of economic assistance.

The man at the pool of Bethesda was perceived by everyone around him to be a victim. As long as he assumed the role of victim, others would feel sorry for him and take care of him. As long as he was paralyzed, he could live off the labor of others because he was not expected to do anything for himself or others. As long as he was perceived to be helpless, he could receive welfare and other forms of public assistance. As long as he was incapacitated, he had an excuse for not coming to church or looking for a job. As long as he was disabled, he did not have to be a father to his children nor a husband to his wife. As long as he was dependent, he could be carried by others.

Conversely, if he got well, he would have to change his whole lifestyle. He would have to get a job and take care of himself. He would be expected to come to church instead of having people visit him and bring lessons to him. He would have to assume responsibility for his wife and children.

There once was a faith healer who had already healed a blind man and a deaf man, and was on the verge of laying hands on a paralytic man to heal him also. Just as the faith healer was about to lay hands on the paralyzed man, he said to the faith healer, "Don't you dare lay hands on me! I am on disability!"

Some of us, in the name of Christian sympathy, are crippling people by allowing them to become or remain dependent upon our assistance. Far too many of us are depending on others to provide support that we should be providing for ourselves. Some of us are making no attempt to become self-reliant and stand on our own two feet. Others claim a disabling condition to justify receiving welfare checks, for accepting hospitality from others, or for receiving charity.

The man at the pool was both an excuser and an accuser. His first "but" was that of an excuser. He gave Jesus a bunch of excuses as to why he had not been healed heretofore. "'Sir,' the paralytic replied, 'I have no one to help me into the pool when the water is stirred'" (John 5:7). He blamed the conditions around the pool for his lack of healing. He made the circumstance seem beyond his control. The paralytic refused to be accountable for his own condition. He refused to accept any responsibility for his quality of life.

The second "but" the paralytic offered was in the form of an accusation. "While I am trying to get in," he explained to Jesus, "someone else goes down ahead of me." He proceeded to blame other people for his condition. It was the fault of others that he had not been healed. The man was still paralyzed because other people managed to get into the pool and get the healing. In this regard, the paralytic was much like people today who blame others for their brokenness.

An alcoholic woman may complain, "If those people on my job didn't get on my nerves so doggone bad, I could quit drinking."

A chronically unemployed man may complain, "Well, they ain't gonna let a black man get one of those jobs."

An overweight woman may reply, "I wouldn't have gained all of this weight if I hadn't had those three babies."

An abusive husband might offer, "I wouldn't hit her if she would just learn to keep the house clean."

Jesus would not accept the paralytic's "buts," neither in the form of excuses nor accusations. Essentially, Jesus told the man to "Get off your butt and take responsibility for your own condition!"

Jesus' command was for the man to literally and figuratively get off of his butt. We cannot always control the circumstances that befall us in life. What we can do, however, is learn to stretch beyond any limitations life may impose. For instance, being born black, female and poor is not an automatic ticket to a lifetime of government subsidy. Being "played" by your woman doesn't mean you have to build emotional walls because you can never trust any woman. Being sexually abused as a child does not mean you will never have a husband or a normal sex life. Being dyslexic doesn't mean a person can't get an education and be successful in life.

When Jesus asked the man if he wanted to be well, he offered Jesus a "but" as an excuse. Basically, the paralytic's response to Jesus was, "I would have been healed already, but I have no one to put me into the pool while the water is stirring." The man wouldn't stop with just one excuse; he offered Jesus two excuses in one sentence. His second reason for not being well was that someone always got in the water ahead of him.

Some people are waiting for the world to stop and allow them to take their time getting into the arena of life and start succeeding. Life stands still for no one. While driving, you may notice that some people sit back in heavy traffic, waiting for someone to stop and let them in. On the other hand, there are drivers who cautiously and respectfully inch into traffic, ready to seize the first opportunity to merge into the flow of traffic. Guess which driver will likely be the first to get into moving traffic? People often react to life in a similar manner. Some people are cautious risk-takers, ready to move and seize an opportunity. Others are like the drivers who sit back and wait...they wait for someone to offer them a job...they wait for someone to notice that they're lonely and looking for someone to date...they wait for someone to stop and notice that they don't have a life!

Because of the excuses the paralytic offered, Jesus knew the man had a need far greater than mobility. The man needed to be made whole—mentally, emotionally, psychologically and physically. The man was in need of spiritual renewal as well as physical healing. Jesus wanted the man to be whole in every way. No healthy person can feel self-gratification while waiting for a welfare check or assistance from others. Continually receiving something for nothing is degrading to the human spirit. Welfare and other assistance does in fact cost something. Eventually, it costs every person who receives it self-esteem and self-respect.

Raising Victims

Not only is our government cultivating victims, some parents are raising victims as well. They are not equipping their children to be responsible adults. Every time a child is pampered by shielding him/her from responsibilities that make him/her strong, the growth of that child is retarded. As the story goes, a boy wrote home from college, "Dear Dad: no mon...no fun...your son." The father wrote back, "So sad...too bad...your Dad...get a job."

This father was teaching his son important principles of self-reliance, just as Jesus helped the man at the pool move beyond victimization to empowerment. The man's response to Jesus was a classic statement of victimization, "I have no one...." From that time until now, these words have been the creed of victims everywhere, "I have no one...." How ironic and tragic to be in the presence of God Incarnate, the Divine Logos, the Renown Healer, Jesus, the Christ, and say, "I have no one...."

Jesus did not respond to the man's self-proclaimed victimization. Jesus refused to commiserate with him. Jesus refused to participate in his pity party. Jesus simply replied, "Rise, take up your bed and walk." In colloquial terms, that means "Get up, go to work, and take care of your own business."

The Church needs to take some lessons from her Head. Too often, in an effort to fulfill our responsibilities as Christians, we get caught up in doing for people instead of enabling people to do for themselves. We buy and distribute fish to the hungry instead of teaching them the skill of fishing. Therefore, the Church sometimes inadvertently creates unhealthy co-dependency, teaching people to be dependent on others instead of modeling dependency on God and interdependence with others.

— *Musings* —

Answer the following questions on a separate sheet of paper. You may also use these questions to stimulate group discussion.

1. By what means are you raising your children to be self-reliant?

2. What past or present situation, circumstance or experience has caused you, or is causing you, to feel and behave like a victim? Examples of victimization include: racism, sexism, ageism, divorce, sickness, poverty, death, recalcitrant children, etc.

3. Do the missions and ministries of your church (or those of most churches) foster victimization or empowerment? Explain your response.

4. If you needed help in the event of an emergency or crisis, where would you go and why? If you would not go to your church or any church for help, elaborate.

5. How might the Church respond in love and compassion to the legitimate needs of the hurting without fostering unhealthy dependency?

6. How might you respond in love and compassion to the legitimate needs of family members and friends without fostering unhealthy dependency?

7. In what ways have African Americans become too dependent on politicians and government to provide for their needs?

8. Why are African Americans disproportionately on welfare and what might the Church do to help reverse this statistic?

9. In what ways or in what areas of your life have you been unnecessarily dependent and how have you been able to overcome those dependencies? Examples of such dependencies include drugs, money, or approval from others.

10. How might the Church employ the methods you suggest to develop effective ministries for creating a sense of self-reliance and personal responsibility?

— Ministries —

A Personal Development Ministry

The purpose of the Personal Development Ministry is to move persons beyond victimology to productive self-reliance so that they might become contributing persons in both Church and society at-large. Victimology is defined as an emotional state of despair and hopelessness due to tragedy or misfortune that causes helplessness to perpetuate and become a way of life.

All persons experience seasons of despair and hopelessness. When hopelessness becomes a way of life, however, impacting our self-perceptions, our conditions, our circumstances, and our opportunities, we have succumbed to victimology.

The Church encounters people on a daily basis who are caught up in victimology. In fact, to some degree, victimology is a disease suffered by everyone on one level or another. For example, a person might be an achiever in his/her professional life, but feel helpless to overcome a weight problem. They may justify their physical state of being to themselves and others by saying such things as, "Everything I eat turns to fat." This is a mild equivalent to what the paralytic man said to Jesus, "I have no one...."

There are varying degrees of victimology, from extreme to mild cases. An example of an extreme case of victimology might be the person who has totally retreated from life due the effects of aging, unresolved grief, shame, deteriorating family relationships or divorce. These kinds of life challenges visit each of us at one time or another, either directly or indirectly. However, perpetual victims allow such challenges to blind them to their hidden strengths and resources. The goal of the Personal Development Ministry is to awaken victims to the healing power of God's love and the inner resources that God gives to the suffering, but to which victimology blinds them.

The Personal Development Ministry is based upon a five-fold strategy:

1. **Training staff and volunteers in detecting victimology in themselves and others.** The following criteria are ways of detecting victimology in others and self:

   - Dwelling on "how bad it is" or "how bad I feel."

   - Looking for handouts and not handups.

   - Making excuses for self-defeating behavior.

   - Retreating from responsibilities.

   - Not taking advantage of personal growth opportunities.

   - Blaming others and God for adverse circumstances.

   - Negative attitude.

   - Finding fault with everyone and everything.

   - Surrounding oneself with negative people.

   - A persistent failure to make a contribution to anything.

   - Over-exaggerating the severity of one's condition.

2. **Personal Development Ministry workshops for staff, congregations and community.**

The goal of the Personal Development Ministry is to help people help themselves. The process begins with helping victims discover what they want for themselves. It is impossible to help someone against his/her will.

If there is a will for healing, the Church must help victimologists discover for themselves their inner and personal resources. The man at the Pool of Bethesda said to Jesus, "I have no one...."

The man, like most victimologists, was guilty of over-exaggerating his condition. The man had many someones, but his own victimology blinded him to Jesus, to fellow sufferers who domiciled with him at the pool, as well as to those who had been carrying him to the pool daily.

3. The Church must help victims complete a self-inventory to discover resources for addressing their own problems.

One way of accomplishing this is through the administration of the "but" test. This test is an adaptation of the apostle Paul's words in 2 Corinthians 4:7-9. Paul proves in this passage that it is possible to be victimized without being a victim. Listen to Paul! "We are troubled but not distressed. Perplexed but not in despair. Persecuted but not forsaken. Cast down but not destroyed." Notice how many times Paul used the word "but" to indicate having risen above personal victimization. In the New Testament, the word "but" is often linked to a positive outcome instead of an excuse for inaction:

> *Troubled, but not distressed....*
> *Perplexed, but not in despair....*
> *Persecuted, but not forsaken....*
> *Cast down, but not destroyed....*

In his book entitled, *Take Comfort* (The Standard Publishing Company, 1991), Bob Russell shares insights concerning our present-day use of the word "but." He observes, "We usually use that word negatively to qualify good things." However, the word is merely a transitional word, yet it is so often used to justify failure, laziness, inactivity, or some other negative consequence.

Every person will experience a time when things do not go as planned. Failures are an integral part of life and are often a part of success. In many instances, a person's failure has become an integral factor leading to victory. When he was in the tenth grade, basketball great Michael Jordan was cut from his high school basketball team. President Abraham Lincoln lost two bids for Congress and two bids for the Senate before being elected president. Albert Einstein was described by his teacher as "mentally slow." Quincy Jones once told Luther Vandross that he would never succeed as a solo artist. Three time Olympic gold medalist Wilma Rudolph was once paralyzed in her left leg. The famous singing group of the 1960's, the Supremes, were once called, "The No Hit Supremes" because their first nine records flopped.

J. Wallace Hamilton once said, "Every man's life is a diary in which he means to write one story but he's forced to write another." Just as Paul used "but" to signal a positive outlook on a negative situation, many people today need learn to how to have such a hopeful orientation toward their circumstances—one that is firmly rooted in faith in Jesus Christ.

To move people beyond victimization, we must help them discover ways of moving beyond the awful things that happen and discover, through God's power, ways of overcoming all of the pains that life inevitably brings. The test, then, for today's overcomers may be:

Unemployed, *but not* _____

Sexually abused, *but not* _____

Unappreciated, *but not* _____

Discriminated against, *but not* _____

Drug addicted, *but not* _____

Single parent, *but not* _____

Helping people to be victorious over the circumstances of life that befall them can be difficult. The circumstances are real and nothing can change that. What can be changed, however, is one's attitude and orientation toward the situation.

4. **Develop a computerized Resource Bank, a collection of social services, community agencies, education and job opportunities that are available in the church and community.**

Every church has resource people who can be tapped to develop services within the church. If the church is unable to provide the ministry or service, the church still can serve as a referral agency. Therefore, in order to have an effective resource bank, it is essential that members of the congregation be encouraged to submit the related information.

The best resource for the resource bank is a mobilized congregation that is alert to available opportunities and services in the community. For example, if members were sensitized to write down all the "help wanted" signs they saw during the course of a week and bring that information to the church's resource bank, the volume would be astounding. News would get out to the community that the church is a place to find employment opportunities.

In his book, *The Local Church in Ministry* (Broadman Press, 1973), William Pinson offers several services that the Church might provide in the resource bank. Under "Needs, Ministries and Resources," he mentions *(other categories included)*:

Aged
Alcoholic
Apartment House Dweller
Autistic
Bereaved
Blind/Vision Impaired
Childless Couples
Deaf/Hearing Impaired
Divorcees
Emotionally Disturbed
Engaged
Ethnic Group Members
Expectant Mothers
Functionally Illiterate
Gangs
Gifted/Talented Child
GLBT Community
Homebound
Homeless
Hospitalized
Housing-Substandard
Hungry
Internationals
Institutionalized
Juvenile Offender
Lonely
Marriage Conflict
Mentally Challenged
Mentally Ill
Migrant Workers
Military Personnel
Narcotic Addict
Neighborhood Residents
Night People
Non-English Speaking
Obese/Eating Disorder
Orthopedically Handicapped
Parent Support
Poor
Prisoner
Released Offender

Resort Area Visitors and Residents	Single Heads of Household
	Slow Learners
Retired Persons	Speech Impaired
Runaway Youth	Suicide/At-Risk
Transition	Unemployed
School Dropouts	Unwed Parents
Sick	Widowed
Single Adults	Youth

5. The Church must help deprogram people out of victimology.

It may seem difficult to believe, but some people must be taught how to hold down a job. After helping multigenerational welfare recipients to get a job, the Church must take its efforts one step farther and teach employment etiquette. Some people who are overweight need to learn about proper nutrition and about the information that the medical community is learning about food and weight. Substance abusers need to learn different ways of coping with stress, anxiety and any other factors that induce reliance on drugs or alcohol. Via anger management techniques, the church can teach many adults who need to know that their spouses or children are not to be used as physical or verbal punching bags.

Dr. W.E.B. Dubois' 1903 classic, *The Souls of Black Folk*, (Signet Classics/Nal Penguin, 1969) includes an essay entitled, "The Faith of Our Fathers," wherein Dubois makes the following observations concerning the pivotal role the African-American church played in the community:

"The Negro Church of today is the social center of Negro life in the United States and the most characteristic expression of African character.... Various organizations meet here; the church proper, the Sunday School and the mass meetings of various kinds. Entertainment, suppers and lectures are held besides the five or six regular weekly religious services. Considerable sums of money are collected and expanded employment is found for the idle, strangers are introduced, news is disseminated and charity distributed. At the same time this social, intellectual and economical center is a religious center of great power."

The church Dubois describes is not one that falsely dichotomized between the secular and the sacred, the spiritual and the physical, the eternal and the temporal. Salvation is always holistic.

There is an African proverb that says, "When you beat one part of the drum, the entire drum vibrates," which is to say that we cannot divorce physical, social and emotional needs from spiritual concerns. What effects one area impacts the whole.

In light of this reality, the Church must diligently help marginalized human beings hopelessly living in the shadows to discover there is yet hope. The good news of the Gospel of Jesus Christ is that no person need remain in his/her current state of misery. To all persons whose lives are unproductive and wasteful, the Church must continue to ask the disturbing question of Jesus, "Wilt thou be made whole?" The follow-up to that question may very well be, "If you do, then get off your but!"

— CHAPTER TWO —

What's Food Got to Do with It?

Daniel made up his mind not to let himself become ritually unclean by eating the food and drinking the wine of the royal court, so he asked Ashpenaz to help him. (Daniel 1:8, GNT)

One of the great performers of the twentieth century was Ethel Waters. She appeared in many Broadway plays and several films during the 1920's, 30's and 40's. In the movie, "Cabin in the Sky", she made the song "His Eye Is on the Sparrow" immortal. Waters, a deeply committed Christian, joined the Billy Graham crusade in the 1960's and became one of the evangelist's featured soloists.

In her autobiography, *To Me, It's Wonderful*, (New York: Harper & Row, 1972) Waters addressed all of the obstacles she had to overcome to achieve success. From first-hand experience, she reflected on poverty, sexism, racism and discrimination. She also shared her experiences with being restricted to certain roles in movies and Broadway musicals because of her race. The greatest battle in her life was not against racism, sexism, or poverty, however. Her greatest struggle was a private battle that she waged and one that remained a secret to the rest of the world. It is a battle that 58 percent of all Americans are presently fighting. The battle that Waters fought is a battle that is becoming an epidemic among African Americans, especially African American females.

What was Ethel Waters most arduous battle? Obesity. When most people think of obesity, we imagine someone of gargantuan size. In fact, obesity is generally defined medically as someone who is more than 20 percent over his/her ideal body weight. Ethel Waters was 200 pounds overweight. At 350 pounds, she had lost the ability to do routine things. Everyday activities became obstacles. She became fatigued from doing simple things like walking, sitting and standing. When she sang, she wore a microphone around her neck because she could not get close enough to a standing microphone because her stomach was too big. She reflected on those days saying, "I hated being fat. I hated myself for being fat and I hated anyone that reminded me that I was fat."

For many overweight persons, the subject of obesity is a very sensitive and emotional issue. Not only do they hate being overweight and hate themselves for being overweight, but they also hate others for reminding them of something about which they feel so powerless. There are many Ethel Waters in our world—people who feel wounded and are carrying within them the pain Ethel Waters knew all too well.

Some may even question why such a topic should be addressed by the Church at all. Is not this a worldly concern? Should not our focus be on spiritual concerns? What relationship does the spa have with spirituality, or Christ with cholesterol? Even those who would make room for health maintenance in the Church give obesity a very marginal place in that room. It is not a primary concern of the average Christian congregation. It's much like singing the National Anthem at a basketball game. Singing the Anthem is not the primary purpose of the gathering, but it is an integral part of the game's opening ceremony. Likewise, health is not the purpose of the Church, but healthy Christians play a pivotal role in the church's ability to accomplish ministry tasks.

Allow me to pose a question. Name one thing you or any believer can effectively do for God without the benefit of good health? Many of the things we are called upon to do for Christ presuppose good health and fitness. It takes more than will and good intentions to do the work of the Lord. It takes healthy bodies. All of our ideas, visions and dreams must be carried out through healthy bodies. Health, diet and nutrition do not fall outside the realm of the Holy. Therefore, nutrition and health literacy are a vital part of Christian education. Next to a good conscience, good health should be every believer's priority. Eating, sleeping and exercising should never be reduced to mere biological functions void of spiritual and moral implications.

For the Hebrews in the Bible, eating is more than merely a biological function; it is a spiritual concern. If I go to McDonald's at noon and buy a Quarter Pounder with cheese, Super Fries and a large Coke, I am just having lunch. When an orthodox Jew patronizes a restaurant, more is involved than eating lunch. The orthodox Jew is engaged in an extension of his/her faith. What and how the orthodox Jew eats is a religious obligation and a form of worship.

This is why the text says that Daniel "purposed in his heart" that he would not defile himself with the king's food. Daniel, along with his three colleagues, were international students whom the Babylonians had deported from Judea to serve in the king's court.

These four students were being groomed in all the ways of the Babylonians. Their minds were being bent to fit Babylonian ideals. They were being reconditioned and indoctrinated into the literature, language and lifestyles of the Babylonians so that they could serve the king. Their names had been changed in order to make them forget their God, their culture, and their country—Daniel was changed to Belteshazzar; Hananiah to Shadrach; Mishael to Meshach; and Azariah to Abednego.

Their final course of training focused on diet. For three years their diets would be closely monitored. The most exquisite and delectable Babylonian cuisines were placed before them. But the text says that Daniel "purposed in his heart not to defile himself" by eating the king's meat. For Daniel, eating was more than a biological function; it possessed religious significance. His diet distinguished him as a member of the Hebrew community. Instead of eating the king's meat, he made a request for vegetables and water. The Babylonians had changed his name, but they could not change his nature. The primary motive behind Daniel's rejection of the Babylonian diet was to maintain cultural and religious distinctiveness. Jews are identified by their diet. The loss of diet means the loss of identity.

On one occasion, a Catholic priest was ribbing his rabbi friend about not eating ham and bacon. The priest said, "Come on, Rabbi, you don't know what you're missing. One taste and you will be hooked. Why would God have created something so delicious if God did not expect people to enjoy it? Come on, Rabbi, when are you finally going to break down and try some?"

The rabbi responded, "I'll try some at your wedding reception." Celibacy helps identify a Catholic priest just much as diet identifies an Orthodox Jew.

As a Christian, you might think that a restricted diet is slavery. Most human beings, Christians included, want to be free to eat all foods. A Jewish person might respond that a restricted diet is a form of slavery that produces freedom, while the alleged "freedom" of an unrestricted diet creates true slavery. Ethel Waters, at 350 pounds, was free to eat any and all that she wanted, but she was not free to breathe, walk, stand, or fit her clothes. She was free to enjoy strokes, heart attacks, diabetes, and kidney disease.

Daniel was identified by his diet. African Americans are identified by our diets. We have maintained our southern traditions of pork chops, chitterlings, country ham, grits, biscuits, fried chicken, and ham hocks. Supermarkets in white suburban communities do not stock the same groceries as the black urban markets. High fat, high salt, and high cholesterol foods reign supreme in the black community. For many, the four basic food groups are fried fish, barbecued ribs, chocolate cake and beer. We fill our plates with foods that clog our arteries and destroy our circulatory system. Before we consume these foods, we pray, asking God to bless our suicide attempts! We are committing suicide with a knife and fork.

African Americans live six years fewer than the national average. We lead the mortality rate in heart disease, cancer, stroke, liver disease, infant mortality, accidental death and homicide. So what's food got to do with it?

The following revision of the twenty-third Psalm reflects current attitudes toward food in this country:

My appetite is my Shepherd. I always want.
It makes me sit down and stuff myself.
It leadeth me to the refrigerator repeatedly.
It leadeth me in the path of Burger King
for a Whopper.
It destroyeth my shape.
Yea though I knoweth I gaineth weight,
I will not stop eating.
For food tastes so good.

The ice cream and cookies, they comfort me.
When the table is spread before me, it
exciteth me, for I knoweth that I shall dig in.
I filleth my plate continuously,
My clothes runneth smaller.
Surely bulges and excess weight shall follow
me all the days of my short life.
And I will dwell in the land of fat forever.

There are all sorts of reasons for our poor diets and undisciplined lifestyles. Sometimes it is due to ignorance. For others it may be caused by stress. When an unhealthy lifestyle is due to stress, the issue is no longer, "What have you been eating?" but "What's been eating you?" Compulsive overeating is often an attempt to satisfy emotional hungers that the person may be unaware he/she has. High calorie foods become a sedative to calm the nerves.

Daniel's diet was nutritionally enriching. The body needs certain nutrients to function at its optimum potential. Throughout the Bible, people ate what nutritionists are now recommending: diets high in fiber and calcium, low in animal fats and with plenty of fresh fruits and vegetables. Read Leviticus 11: consumption of animal fats that contribute to high cholesterol is limited.

In the Bible, all of the breads are made from whole grains. Jacob fixed Esau pottage, or lentil soup. The ten spies brought back a cluster of grapes to demonstrate the prosperity of Canaan. Jesus fed the multitude with loaves of bread made from barley and fish. The father of the prodigal son celebrated the return of his son with the killing of the fatted calf, not the fatted pig. Christ served his followers grilled fish at the first breakfast after His resurrection.

The people of the Bible exercised. Daniel and Jesus exercised, but not in a fitness center. They walked everywhere, pumped water, chopped wood, and stoked fires, all of which are cardiovascular activities.

In the verses beginning with the first chapter of Daniel, we find the four essentials that we need in order to maintain a healthy lifestyle. First, we need a made up mind. The text says, Daniel made up his mind that he would not defile himself by eating from the king's table. A made up mind is essential. Only the individual can make a decision about adopting proper exercise and good nutrition as a way of life.

Second, eating must be a form of worship and honor to God. Daniel worshiped God by what he ate. Eating must be a matter of worship. We need to honor God by what we eat. Jesus warned against praying vain prayers. A vain prayer is one that petitions God to bless the unhealthy food you are about to eat—food that can kill you. Only ask God to bless food that is going to bless you, physically and spiritually.

Third, a person who struggles with eating right and exercising regularly needs a support group. Daniel developed a health conscious fellowship; he was not alone. He said, "Give us vegetables and water." He had a support group made up of Shadrach, Meshach and Abednego. A support group helps members resist the media's bombardment of messages encouraging people to eat unhealthy foods in an undisciplined manner. The media's emphasis is on quantity because the more you eat the more they sell. A 7-Eleven, Double Gulp Coke has 768 calories. McDonald's Super-fries have 540 calories. A king-sized Butterfinger has 510 calories. A person who is an overeater needs a fellowship to develop and maintain good eating habits.

The media also makes you think you are hungry when you are not. The media also gives a message that you will not gain weight by eating the foods they advertise. Commercials for high-calorie foods do not feature overweight people. The people who appear in fast food and junk food advertisements are slender and healthy-looking. By doing so, advertisers give a subtle message that eating the advertised food will not cause weight gain. A support group will help overeaters stay focused in the face of media mis-representations about food and eating.

Finally, our diet must become a lifestyle choice. Daniel's intake of vegetables and water was not a diet; it was a way of life. Daniel and his boys did not eat vegetables and water for ten days and then go on a binge of the king's food for ten days. Theirs was a lifestyle.

The superintendent over Daniel and his friends granted his request. For ten days, Daniel and his friends were able to eat their requested regimen of vegetables and water. Everyone else was eating at Ryan's, White Castle, and McDonald's, while Daniel and his friends ate green beans, blueberries, broccoli, cabbage, cantaloupe, carrots, cauliflower, cherries, grapes, lemons, lettuce, nectarines, watermelon, spinach, strawberries, and tomatoes, and so forth.

At the end of the ten-day period, the results were unquestionable. The Hebrew boys, with their regimen of vegetables and water, were healthier and more handsome than those who had consumed the king's diet. The supervisor was convinced. He allowed the Hebrew boys to continue their chosen diet. When their three years of preparation were completed, the king met with them for personal interviews. He found Daniel and his friends to be physically fit, attractive, mentally alert and ready for service.

What's food got to do with it? Our diets prepare us for service. When Ethel Waters was 200 pounds overweight, she could barely sing, breathe, walk, sit or function. So she prayed. God had so much for her to do—songs to sing, burdens to lift and hearts to encourage. Unfortunately, she could not stop eating; that is, until someone told her that if she was hungry for more than what her body needed, she was not really hungry for food. Her true hunger was for fellowship with God. At age 57, Waters lost 200 pounds and lived many more years to sing, to serve, to bless, to heal, to help, to give hope, and to tell the world that God's eye is on the sparrow.

What's food got to do with it? By November 1987, Mayor Harold Washington had electrified politics in Chicago. He had unified the community. No one could stop him—not Richard Daley or Michael A. Bilandic or Jane Byrne. Unfortunately, he led a fast-paced, undisciplined life—running from meeting to meeting, mediating strikes and city council wars, and staying up late to catch up on his reading. At 5'10" tall, he weighed 265 pounds—80 pounds over his ideal weight. He smoked cigarettes for over thirty years. Both his blood pressure and cholesterol were high. He often canceled appointments with doctors because he felt other business was more pressing. He canceled a doctor's appointment in November of 1987. On the very day he canceled his appointment, he had a fatal heart attack.

God had so much for him to do in areas of improved housing, job programs, anti-slum programs, youth and gang violence and education. There was so much for him to do, yet he may never have realized that food was partially the reason why he departed this life with unfinished business.

Do you want to help your family? If so, food has something to do with it. Do you want to preach a sermon? If you do, food has something to do with it. Do you want to sing a song? Then food has something to do with it. No matter what you want to do for the Lord, that work can be affected by your relationship with food.

— *Musings* —

Answer the following questions on a separate sheet of paper. You may also use these questions to stimulate group discussion.

1. Do a quick inventory of your personal eating habits. How much high fat, over-processed food do you eat versus high fiber, simply cooked or uncooked foods recommended to maintain good health?

2. What snack foods do you consume most often?

3. Under what conditions do you find yourself eating improperly?

4. What lifestyle modifications do you need to make in order to facilitate better nutrition (e.g. carrying snacks and lunch to work, etc.)?

5. Do you have a nutritional support system to help you stay on track?

6. What kind of food support system would make maintaining good eating habits more effective for you?

7. Do your eating habits reflect the media's influence?

8. If you were selected to plan the next church supper, what menu would you propose that supports principles of good nutrition?

9. If you are a parent, how are you helping to develop Daniel's sense of purpose with regard to your child(ren)'s nutrition?

10. List your greatest personal challenges for nutritional health and commit them to prayer.

— *Ministries* —

Christercise Fitness Program

To better discern God's will for His life, Jesus entered into a comprehensive health and nutrition program. Some may question whether health and nutrition are appropriate terms in describing this very familiar incident. However, Jesus realized the inter-connectedness between good health and spiritual fitness. Matthew records that Jesus engaged in activities that even modern nutritionists would say promote good health. It included a good diet, a positive attitude, goal setting, consistency, and discipline.

St. Stephen Baptist Church Family Life Center has patterned a fitness program after the example of Jesus—one we are confident will help us to be fit vessels in the service of our Lord. The "Christercise" Ministry is an observation for Lent and beyond. (This information can easily be placed in brochure form to help publicize the ministry at your church).

Christercise meets at St. Stephen on Mondays, Tuesdays, and Thursdays from 6:00–7:00 p.m. Educational and nutritional talks are held during the forty days and nights of Lent. During the six-week program participants will have cholesterol and blood pressure screening. Participants are encouraged to think of something to give up for Lent.

Your church may also distribute the following information to promote Christercise or another ministry related to health and good nutrition. If your church cannot establish a customized ministry for health and nutrition, consider sponsoring an existing program, such as Weigh Down Workshop, Overeaters Anonymous or Overeaters Victorious. There may be others in your area. Consult a community newspaper or check the Yellow Pages for more information on nutrition from a Christian perspective. Visit your local Christian bookstore for materials and guidebooks to help those who consume food excessively or have an eating disorder. Many self-help materials are now available.

Importance of Weight Control

Years ago, being overweight was considered a sign of success and prosperity. A man who was fortunate enough to provide himself and his family with an abundance of food let obesity speak for his comfortable position in life. At the same time, plumpness was thought to enhance a woman's charm and appearance.

It is not so today. We now know that an overweight person is not necessarily well-nourished or healthy. Current knowledge of what contributes to good health and long life makes it clear that obesity is a serious deterrent, not a contributor, to good health. Excess poundage puts undue strain on the human body. Statistics show that people who are very overweight appear to be more susceptible to certain diseases, have shorter life expectancies, may have less resistance to infection, and even tend to have more accidents than persons of ideal body weight.

Aside from these persuasive arguments for attaining and maintaining normal weight, there is the full-length mirror to face and last year's suit to fit into! More important, when we are physically fit, we are more able to do the work of our Lord and Savior.

How much more comfortable many of us would feel, both inside and out, if we could say "get lost" or "presto" and lose those excess pounds. But it's not that easy. It takes time and patience to lose those extra pounds. Getting rid of extra pounds need not be too difficult—if it's accomplished little by little, following the Christercise Fitness Program.

Expectations

- Pray every day.
- Attend weekly meetings.

- You must give up something—such as a favorite food, activity, or habit—the absence of which entails personal sacrifice.

- Practice reciprocity—try to give and receive with an open heart and mind.

- Make sure that there is continuous love in your life. Make family/relationships a priority.

- Sunday School attendance is mandatory!!!

Diet/Exercise/Health

- Remember, the goal of eating is not taste, but nutrition.

- Get six to eight hours of sleep each night.

- Bathe or shower every day—seek cleanliness.

- Monitor caloric intake.

- Quit or significantly reduce smoking.

- Do not consume alcoholic beverages. Exercise daily for a minimum of one hour.

- Start each day with 15 minutes of deep breathing; try to bring life-giving oxygen into your stomach.

- Drink eight glasses of water per day. (Remember that eight glasses a day keeps the fat away.)

- Eat only between 6:00 a.m. and 7:00 p.m.

Readings

- Read selected Bible passages.

- Read prayers from the Bible.

- Read something on the subject of world peace.

- Read something concerning world hunger.

- Engage in an activity that will enhance your knowledge of and commitment to justice concerns.

- Be disciplined. You must read at least one book during the forty-day Lenten season.

Keep a Daily Journal

- Log your feelings in a journal. Pay special attention to times when you want to overeat. Does your desire to eat occur at a certain time of day? What are your feelings at the times you want to overeat?

- Log your shortcomings. Take a personal inventory of your own character flaws and sinful behaviors that need to be addressed through confession, prayer and repentance.

- Include a list of persons who have been harmed by your negative behavior. Apologize or make restitution to all those you have harmed.

Penalties

You should be willing to pay one dollar ($1.00) or bring one canned good each time you break a requirement. Example: You drank only five glasses of water in one day instead of the recommended eight glasses. This requires personal honesty and commitment. Fulfilling the program requirements and being honest when you do not fulfill them will only aid in individual success.

— UnderPound Railroad Program —

This program is offered as an alternative program to provide ongoing support for those who eat compulsively, binge eat, or who otherwise have maintained a pattern of unhealthy eating habits. The Underpound Railroad Program of Nutrition (URPN) is designed to help persons escape their bondage to overeating, unhealthy eating or poor eating habits and enter into a lifestyle of freedom that accompanies a disciplined plan of eating.

Chief Conductor — this person coordinates the work of the URPN. This person must be committed to a healthy lifestyle—one that extends beyond eating habits and exercise. Ideally, the Chief Conductor has overcome obesity, a pattern of compulsive eating or poor eating habits. The Chief Conductor must not take a judgmental approach to his/her post. Rather, this person must view his/her role as that of one who facilitates the success of those in the program. The Chief Conductor is the strategist who develops plans to keep the Underpound Railroad functional at all levels.

Conductors — these persons serve as motivators, guides and advisors to those who have joined the URPN because they desire freedom from obesity and/or a lifestyle of unhealthy eating. Conductors should have a zeal for helping others overcome compulsive eating or a lifestyle of unhealthy eating habits. Conductors must have a willing heart and ears, keeping in mind that participants may, at times, share information of a highly personal nature. Those who cannot maintain confidentiality should not agree to serve as a Conductor. Ideally, Conductors are persons who have overcome obesity, a pattern of compulsive eating, poor eating habits, or some other compulsive/addictive or destruction pattern of behavior.

Liberators — those who recognize that they have a pattern or lifestyle of overeating, yo-yo dieting, binge eating (and perhaps purging), or unhealthy eating habits. Liberators must join the program by personal decision because they believe in the program and want to be helped. No one should be forced to enter the program through guilt or coercion. Liberators must be willing to abide by the program's philosophy.

Guidelines for
Underpound Railroad Program

- Liberators should recognize and admit that food/eating has posed a personal problem and has inhibited the quality of their lives.

- Liberators should recognize that their ongoing problem with food/eating indicates there are other, perhaps hidden, issues to be addressed.

- Liberators, Conductors and other participants should be committed to a lifestyle of honesty, especially in the context of group meetings.

- Liberators should never be subject to embarrassment or humiliation in conjunction with any part of the program.

- Every Liberator should be encouraged to call his/her Conductor and other Liberators when tempted to overeat or retreat to old behaviors.

- Meetings should be available no less than once each week. If possible, use your network of Conductors to facilitate several meetings each week.

- Open meetings to the community at-large. Especially encourage persons who are unchurched to attend.

- Conductors must recognize when a Liberator is grappling with an issue that requires professional help and be prepared to take appropriate action.

- Develop a network of caring, Christian professionals who can help Liberators and their families cope with sensitive or difficult issues.

- The Underpound Railroad should guide Liberators to the understanding that, through Christ, they can do all things.

- Begin every meeting with prayer.

- At every meeting, affirm Philippians 4:13, "I can do everything through him who gives me strength" (NIV).

- During meetings, Conductors and Liberators should not offer advice to one another. Each participant should address his/her personal issues. A Liberator seeking the advice of a Conductor should do so before or after the meeting.

- Conductors serve to open and close meetings. Conductors also monitor talk during meetings so that no one participant dominates the meeting nor gives advice or judgment.

- Conductors help to create an open environment in which Liberators can talk freely without fear of judgment or condemnation.

- Attendance at meetings should be limited to Liberators and Conductors. If needed, a meeting for Liberators and their families should be established.

- Conductors should be interviewed carefully by the Chief Conductor before agreeing to serve.

As your church develops it own Underpound Railroad Program of Nutrition, you may need to make adjustments to fit the needs of those who attend at your church.

— CHAPTER THREE —

Give Me a Break!

Observe the Sabbath and keep it holy. You have six days in which to do your work, but the seventh day is a day of rest dedicated to me. On that day no one is to work–neither you, your children, your slaves, your animals, nor the foreigners who live in your country. (Exodus 20:8-10, GNT)

• • • • • •

Come to me, all of you who are tired from carrying heavy loads, and I will give you rest. Take my yoke and put it on you, and learn froom me, because I am gentle and humble in spirit; and you will find rest. For the yoke I will give you is easy, and the load I will put n you is light. (Matthew 11:28-30, GNT)

Some time ago, I conducted an informal survey of 100 Christians attending a mid-week Bible study. The purpose of the survey was to determine the five most sacred activities in a Christian's life. The responses I received were all good, but predictable. At the top of the list were prayer, Bible study, witnessing, fasting, and tithing.

There were other activities mentioned; however, one activity was omitted from everyone's list—rest! I was not surprised that rest was not present among the top five of anyone's list. In fact, I would have been surprised if someone had written it down. We tend not to think of rest as being spiritual activity. We would not group rest with prayer, meditation, witnessing and worship.

While vacationing with my family in Orlando, Florida one summer, I happened to see a man lying on a lawn chair by the pool at our hotel. I noticed that he was reading a book with the intriguing title, *When I Relax, I Feel Guilty*. As I watched that obviously relaxed guy, two thoughts came to mind. The first was, "Gee, I'll bet you feel guilty right now." The second was, "That book is the story of my life."

Not only is rest disregarded as a spiritual activity, but we sometimes feel guilty about resting to receive its physical and emotional benefits. The reason is because we have lost sight of what the Bible says about rest. While those in the survey did not mention rest, their omission was not because the Bible does not mention it. The Bible makes reference to some form of rest 168 times. These passages address the importance of finding a resting place or the importance of restfulness.

The Bible teaches us that God intends for us to punctuate our busy schedules with periods of rest. Therefore, rest is a spiritual activity. In fact, God first showed us the example by resting Himself. After six days of creative activity, God rested on the seventh day. This depiction in the Old Testament contains some of the most engaging anthropomorphic words ever attributed to God.

A resting God reveals to us the true rhythm of life. God was showing the way that life was intended to be lived—times of work, punctuated with periods of rest. Therefore, "Give me a break!" may be a very spiritual request and not simply an idiom. God not only rested, but God commanded that we, too, observe a day of rest. God said, "Six days shall you labor, but on the Sabbath day, rest." Sabbath is the special word in the Bible for rest. The word Sabbath means "to stop, to cease, or to be still." It is God's will that we Sabbath, or be still, rest, take a break.

Rest is as necessary to life as work. Rest was not conceived by a lazy, inactive, idle underachiever. Rest was God's idea. Rest was not an afterthought of God, nor a delayed addendum. Rest is an integral part of God's plan for our lives to insure our wholeness and well-being.

In the New Testament, Jesus echoed the same message. Jesus' greatest controversies with the religious leadership of His day centered on the Sabbath or the day of rest. Jesus said, "God gave us the Sabbath to benefit us." It is God's will that we Sabbath. Only when work and rest are held in proper balance is real health possible.

This is how Jesus lived. There was a rhythm to Jesus' life. He would engage in helpful service with people; then He would disengage for a period of rest. Jesus' life was not lopsided—all work and no rest nor all rest and no work. There was a rhythmic pattern to his lifestyle. He would engage and disengage. He would encounter the hurts of people, and then He would escape for rest. His relentless ministry was always followed by restful solitude. Jesus took a break.

The Gospel of Mark captures the work-rest rhythm in the life of Jesus. In the city of Capernaum, Jesus taught and healed the sick. After a day of heavy activity, He retreated to a lonely place for rest and relaxation. The multitude, including His disciples, were unable to find Him. Jesus left everyone and ceased all communication with others. In modern terms, that means He turned off His computer, tablet, and cell phone and left town for a few days.

Jesus knew something that we all need to discover. The quality of our service to others depends on what we have to offer. The demands of life are energy consuming. Therefore, we have to be renewed through rest. Rest revitalizes, rejuvenates and refreshes the nervous system.

Many of us are tugged back and forth between business commitments and family responsibilities. If we devote attention to respond to the needs of our children or spouses, we are made to feel guilty about neglecting our jobs. When we respond to the demands and pressures of work, we feel guilty about neglecting our families. On those rare occasions when we are able to juggle both family and work, the church shows up to encourage us to get involved in ministries like Sunday School, Bible study, choir rehearsal, visiting the sick, and evangelizing the lost. We get worn out and sometimes burned out because of the ever sprawling demands placed on us. We cry out, "Give me a break!"

Talk with anyone and it's the same old story. Everyone is not only tired, but in the words of the late Civil Rights activist Fannie Lou Hamer, they are "...sick and tired of being sick and tired." Our calendars are full, our schedules are overcrowded, our responsibilities are excessive, and expectations of us are high. We are overbooked, over committed, overextended and overexerted. Our energies are depleted and our strength is drained. Our heads hurt, blood pressure is up, patience is low, anger is quick, our families are disintegrating, and we ourselves are about to snap.

Dr. William A. Jones, pastor of Bethany Baptist Church in Brooklyn, New York, asserts that the reason African Americans do not attend PTA meetings, vote or volunteer is because we are a tired people. After catching the bus to shuttle back and forth between two jobs, feed the family, and work with our own children, African Americans are exhausted. We need a break. This is especially true of African American females who sometimes have to be both mother and father to their children. Many lack any kind of support—financial, emotional or otherwise. This creates frustrations that can serve as the breeding ground for problems like drug and alcohol abuse, domestic violence, child neglect and even child abuse.

In some form or fashion, all of us need to give ourselves a break. In other words, "Stop before you drop." People will say and do things when they are tired that they would not say or do when they are properly rested. Fatigue is like a drug. Fatigue dulls the mind, weakens the will, fuels incoherence, destroys morale, and makes us irritable and quick to lose our tempers.

In the English language, there is something called a run-on sentence. These are sentences that just keep going without some form of punctuation for pause or closure, such as a comma, semi-colon, period, question mark, or exclamation point. Sentences must come to closure; they cannot just keep going. In order to communicate effectively, language must allow for pauses and closures. In music, there something called a rest. The key to making good music is not simply knowing how to play or sing, but when to pause and rest. Most building codes require electrical devices called circuit breakers. Circuit breakers prevent a load of energy from overloading the circuits that can lead to a melt down and cause fires.

Just as there is punctuation in our language to prevent run-on sentences, and rest in music to facilitate tempo and harmony, and circuit breakers in buildings to prevent fires caused by electrical overloads, every aspect of life needs punctuation, rest and circuit breakers.

There are no substitutes for rest. Stimulants like coffee, chocolate, cola, and pills produce only artificial energy and will never be a substitute for the divinely-implanted need for rest. Using a stimulant is like starting a car, putting it in neutral, and stepping on the gas pedal. The engine is being worked, but the car is not going anywhere. If we rely on stimulants to keep us going, we may feel like we have lots of energy, but in reality we're not really going anywhere.

If we would only take breaks, our minds would be more alert, our bodies would be healthier, and we would have more energy for facing the demands of life. This truth illustrates how God's commands are rooted in Scripture and all of our realities. We do not break the Ten Commandments; rather, we break ourselves when we do not obey them.

Common Reasons Why People Avoid Taking a Break

1. Trying to Live Life All at Once

We often place upon ourselves pressures to achieve much in a very short period of time. Everything is accelerated. Some of us even stand in front of a microwave oven saying, "Won't you hurry up?"

Warning: instant achievement and overnight success has its hazards. An accelerated pace is not necessarily God's will and may reflect spiritual immaturity. God is a God of patience and proper timing. One day is like a thousand years and a thousand years is like one day. It is God's will that we slow down and spread our life plans and activities over a period of time.

Jet lag is the fatigue we feel when we cross time zones in accelerated travel. The body arrives in a new time zone; however, our biological clock is not there yet. Therefore, the internal body clock has to catch up with the physical body. Many people are experiencing life lag. We have often arrived at goals too fast, and our minds, bodies and souls have not had a chance to catch up.

2. Greed and Covetousness

Dr. Wayne Oates, professor of psychiatry and behavioral sciences at the University of Louisville, tells of a man who had a nervous breakdown and had to be hospitalized during World War II. Dr. Oates went to visit the man who then told Dr. Oates that he was being paid back because of his sins. Dr. Oates asked, "What sins?" The man responded, "I work in the munitions plant. Because many able-bodied men were away at war, there was a lot of overtime to work. I worked overtime and double shifts. Because I did, I ended up in here. So the Lord made me lie down."

Jesus asked the question, "What does it profit a man to gain the whole world and lose his soul [self]?" Essentially, what does it profit a person to work incessantly and own a big luxurious house, but never be home to enjoy it? What does it profit a person to make a lot of money, but lose one's family in the process? Jesus said, "Life does not consist of the abundance of the things we possess."

3. The Messiah Complex

The Messiah Complex is the feeling that we can save the world, carry everyone's burden, and straighten out everyone else's problems. When a person is battling the Messiah Complex, self is neglected because the person feels that God wants him/her to sacrifice personal well-being for the sake of others. Everyone else's needs take priority over personal needs, including the need for rest and renewal.

When a person has the Messiah Complex, he or she becomes the one whom everyone approaches, saying "Excuse me, but would you do me a small favor?" or "I know it's your day off, but this is an emergency." You never respond with "no." Because you never say "no" to lesser things, you have no energy for greater things.

In her book, *When Helping You Is Hurting Me: Escaping the Messiah Trap* (HarperCollins, 1988), Carman Renee Berry identifies seven types of messiahs: Messiah Pleaser, Messiah Rescuer, Messiah Giver, Messiah Counselor, Messiah Protector, Messiah Teacher, and Messiah Crusader.

The Messiah Trap leads to "helpaholism." In order to be approved and accepted by everyone, those caught in the trap go out of their way to be the messiah of others. Helpaholism can also be present in religion. We work ourselves to death seeking to be approved by God. It was helpaholism that prompted Jesus to make the most important statement in the Bible concerning rest.

Jesus looked into the tired faces of people who were killing themselves in an attempt to make themselves more acceptable to God. The religious leadership of Jesus' day had established a lot of rules and regulations that the Jewish community believed had to be followed in order to win God's favor. These rules were heavy burdens. Jesus offered them an alternative vision: "Come unto me all you who are under a burden, and I will give you rest. Take my yoke upon you and learn of me. I am meek and lowly in heart and you will find rest for your souls, for my yoke is easy and my burdens are light."

4. Poor Burden Management

Contrary to popular belief, Christianity is not a burden free faith, and Christians do not lead burden free lives. Unlike many Eastern religions, which make the elimination of burdens the goal of life (Nirvana), Christianity recognizes that burdens are unavoidable and, to a great degree, necessary for spiritual growth. The goal of the Christian faith is not the elimination of burdens, rather the proper management of them.

The word stress is being tossed around in the mental health community. However, the term stress is not really a clinical term. The word stress is borrowed from the architectural community. When structural engineers design buildings, they must determine the stress capacity of walls, floor and ceilings. If the engineer overloads a ceiling beyond its stress capacity, the ceiling will cave in, perhaps destroying the entire structure.

We are similarly designed. When our lives are loaded down with too many burdens, life as we know it collapses. We can only accommodate so much emotional and psychological weight before we snap. According to Dr. Henry Mitchell, one of the characteristics of Soul Religion is the belief that God "won't put more us than we can bear." However, many African Americans sometimes wonder if God is a poor Engineer who has miscalculated the stress capacity of darker hued people.

God will not put more on us than we are able to bear, however, if we exercise proper burden management. The Bible teaches three things about burden management.

Bear Them — "Every person should bear his/her own burden" (Galatians 6:5 Paul employs the use of a military word picture. Each soldier is given a backpack (burden) with provisions. Each soldier is to carry his/her own backpack. Each soldier is able to carry his/her own backpack, but if a soldier is burdened down with the backpacks of others, the soldier will exceed his or her stress capacity. Therefore, the art of burden management requires that each individual sort out backpacks, making friends, family, employers, and church members responsible for carrying their own backpack (burdens).

This is especially true in the Church. Many members are overtaxed and overworked because of the "comfortable pew" syndrome. The "comfortable pew" syndrome occurs when members sit comfortably in their pews without taking responsibility for the development and advancement of the church. This creates proxy religion, whereby they depend on others to do what they should be doing themselves. Proxy religion is an abomination. Paul says, "Every man (adult) must carry his (her) own backpack." In fact, Paul seems to be defining maturity as the ability to carry one's own backpack.

Share Them — "Bear one another's burdens" (Galatians 6:2). There is no contradiction between bearing one another's burdens and every person bearing his/her own burden. No one is absolved from dealing with his/her own personal burdens. Rather, this verse simply recognizes that some burdens are communal and social in nature. Just as some songs are composed to be sung by a soloist, there are other songs that can only be sung effectively by a collection of voices operating in harmony and unity. It would be difficult if not impossible to sing "The Hallelujah Chorus" as a solo.

African Americans would be less fatigued individually if we would learn to work communally more often. If we ever learn to trade with each other, network among each other, form food and clothing coops, credit unions, block watch clubs and live out the spirit of *ujamaa* (cooperative economics), we could truly say, "God won't put more on you than you are able to bear."

Transfer Them — "Cast your burdens upon the Lord and He shall sustain thee" (Psalm 55:22). Nothing interferes with rest like worry and anxiety. Jesus said, "Do not be anxious."

Anxiety-free living should not be confused with detached nonchalance or denial. There is a difference between worry and concern. Christians can and should be concerned. Concern is proactive, while worry is a fruitless exercise of the mind that keeps thoughts revolving endlessly without action. Christian author Leslie Weatherhead says that worry is like racing an automobile engine without letting in the clutch—one wastes both gasoline and energy without ever moving.

There are burdens in the form of worry and anxiety that we need to leave with God. We must believe that God will provide and take care of those things that we cannot handle. So many times the things we worry about never happen. When they do happen, God's grace is sufficient for dealing with those circumstances.

Learning techniques for burden management helps to eliminate two major sleep disorders: fatigue and insomnia. Fatigue is the depletion of physical energies due to worry, stress, anxiety and sin. One of the negative consequences of sin is that it drains us of energy. The worry that results from sin drains us of physical and emotional vitality.

When the prophet Jonah tried to escape God's assignment, he sought refuge on a boat. As he was hiding, a storm arose. In the midst of the storm, Jonah went to sleep. The sleep that Jonah was experiencing, however, was not the restful peace of a clear conscious. Jonah's fatigue was the result of depleted energy due to sin and disobedience.

Insomnia is another sleep disorder caused by the mismanagement of burdens. Insomnia is not a disease itself; rather it is a symptom of stress and anxiety. Insomnia can manifest itself in three ways: difficulty falling asleep; difficulty staying asleep; or waking up too soon.

Insomnia and fatigue should not be considered physical diseases. Instead they are the symptoms of something good or bad taking place in your life. For example, children often are unable to sleep when they anticipate something special in the morning, such as the night before Christmas. They are experiencing a form of insomnia. Anxiety about issues such as bills, work, guilt, racism and children can hinder sleep. A classic biblical example of insomnia is King Xerxes in the Book of Esther (Esther 6:1-10). King Xerxes was unable to sleep until he corrected a wrong that he had committed.

Even when medication is prescribed for insomnia, the medication only dulls the mind regarding the stresses that prevent sleep. Medication causes the mind to shut down. However, whenever the mind is shut down from receiving negative messages, the mind also remains closed to positive messages. One of the goals of Christian ministry is to enable people to rest by relieving the worries and anxieties that produce stress. A prime of example of this is Peter on the eve of his planned execution. The apostle James had already been executed, and King Herod Agrippa intended to execute Peter the following morning. Peter was chained between two guards, with two additional guards serving as watchmen over those guards. Nevertheless, Luke records, Peter was asleep. Peter was not sedated by Valium, nor was he tranquilized. He experienced the peace of God that the apostle Paul addressed in the Book of Philippians.

Give me a break! The problem with the request is that it places the spirituality of rest in the hands of others. The very wording implies that the ability to obtain a break does not rest within the person who needs it. If a person will allow it, other people will continue to let that person serve as the messiah for everyone and break down as a lonely helpaholic. Rest will only come when one recognizes that he/she has a right to rest. The command to rest must be obeyed, no matter how urgent the surrounding issues and concerns may seem.

There was woman whose husband was gravely ill. The doctor, who was prone to hyperbole, told his wife in a private consultation that if she did not work, clean, scrub, cut the grass, wash, iron, fold the clothes, keep the children, prepare meals and serve them to her husband in bed, her husband might get worse and die. After the consultation, the sick husband asked his wife what the doctor had said. She replied, "The doctor said you are going to die." The wife refused to serve as her husband's messiah, breaking herself down to fix whatever ailed him.

There are many urgent issues confronting Christians today. Because Christians are prone to be altruistic, we often are guilty of helping others at the expense of our own health and even our spiritual well-being. The call to rest is a call from God. Rest is as much a part of discipleship as prayer, worship, tithing and witnessing. Rest is spiritual activity. Therefore, anything that robs us of securing our fair and needed share of rest is a sin. Therefore, we cannot simply demand that others "Give me a break!" Instead, we are called upon to take a break in Jesus' name.

— *Musings* —

Answer the following questions on a separate sheet of paper. You may also use these questions to stimulate group discussion.

1.   Why is rest not perceived as a spiritual activity?

2.   List some of the things that the local church does to inadvertently foster workaholism?

3.   What would you tell a person who works two jobs as a necessity concerning his/her need for rest?

4.   What are some of the things you are doing to obey God's command to rest?

5.   In what ways are you guilty of one or more of the Messiah Trap characteristics?

6.   How can you begin to practice proper burden management in your life right away?

7.   How can Christians encourage people to rest without breeding laziness and sloth?

— *Ministries* —

You may want to give the following quiz to help identify persons who may benefit from a ministry that aids in facilitating rest and burden management.

Insomnia Quiz

Circle the statements that apply to you:

1.   Falling asleep is hard for me.

2.   I have too much on my mind to go to sleep.

3. When I wake up in the middle of the night, I can't go back to sleep.

4. I can't relax because I have too many worries.

5. Even when I sleep through the night, I'm still tired in the morning.

6. Sometimes I am afraid to close my eyes and go to sleep.

7. I often wake up too early.

8. It takes me more than an hour to fall asleep.

9. I am stiff and sore in the morning.

10. I feel depressed when I can't sleep.

If you circled...

- One to three statements: you are experiencing normal sleeping patterns or have occasional trouble sleeping, which is also normal.

- Four to six statements: You are experiencing some problems with sleep.

- Seven to ten statements: You may have a sleep problem or disorder that requires medical attention.

Fatigue and Rest

One of the important issues related to fatigue is its origin. Contrary to popular belief, fatigue is not caused by mere physical and mental exertion. Physical and mental exertion are most often the consequences of other issues that have not been resolved in our lives, such as unhealthy lifestyles and values.

For example, if we experience fatigue and burnout because we are constantly expending our mental and physical energies resolving the problems of others, the origin of this fatigue may be codependency. Codependency occurs when we overextend ourselves and allow ourselves to be absorbed in the problems of others in order to be loved and accepted by them. A classic example of codependency can be found the old Starkist tuna commercials. If you remember, there was a fish named Charlie Tuna who was trying constantly to be accepted by Starkist. In every commercial, Charlie Tuna was doing something (learning golf, going to the opera...) in an attempt to make himself acceptable to Starkist. Charlie Tuna was a driven fish, constantly on the move because he wanted acceptance from a source that constantly rejected him. In spite of what Charlie did, it was not enough because, as the saying went, "Sorry Charlie, Starkist doesn't want Tuna with good taste. Starkist wants tuna that tastes good!"

A lot of people are like Charlie Tuna. Their Starkist may be a parent, a spouse, friends, children, or even church. The need to be accepted often causes us to work when we should be still, thus violating God's command that we rest.

Many Christians are unaware of the force that is driving them. Therefore, it would be very helpful if the Church offered a seminar on "Healthy Lifestyles." A healthy lifestyle seminar should address common "rest robbers" that deplete our energies and make us ineffective in pursuing God's will for our lives. As a strong advocate of Sunday School, I highly recommend this seminar be held during the Sunday School hour.

1. Workaholism

A lifestyle dominated by the need to earn approval and worth through work and/or productivity. The workaholic believes "I can never do enough, and what has been done is not good enough to warrant rest."

Another belief common to workaholics is, "No one else can do this job as effectively as I can." It would be an interesting exercise to go to a cemetery and find out what occupation each person buried there held during his/her lifetime. A follow up to the deceased person's former employers would probably reveal that, with rare exception, someone else was indeed able to effectively take over the job.

A biblical example of a workaholic can be found in Martha (Luke 10:38-42). Read this familiar Bible story and discuss the following questions concerning the roots of workaholism.

Questions for Discussion on Workaholism

a. In what way is Martha an example of workaholism?

b. Was Martha's desire to please Jesus, a works-oriented type of salvation?

c. In this same chapter is the familiar story of the Good Samaritan. Is it possible that Luke was trying to strike a balance between the service of the Good Samaritan and being spiritually refreshed, like Mary?

d. In what ways has Martha's kind of workaholism contributed to psychological problems such as misconceptions, excessive worry, distorted thinking, inappropriate emotional expression, disorientation, pacing, nail biting, and inappropriate ways of relating to others?

e. What effects—physical, emotional, and spiritual—might Martha's stress have had on her, for instance, blood pressure, gastrointestinal changes (ulcers), or a breakdown in the immune system to fight off illness?

f. How did Jesus help Martha to move beyond workaholism and discover rest through His unconditional acceptance?

2. PowerThirst

This is a lifestyle dominated by an unhealthy compulsion to get ahead, to gain money, power, and fame. Sociologist Tony Campolo calls it "The Success Fantasy." The success fantasy consists of wealth, power and prestige. These three factors are used by society as the criteria for success. The desire to have these things at the expense of our physical and emotional well being, our families, and our spiritual development is idolatry. A biblical example of this can be found in the story of the Rich Young Ruler (Luke 18:18-30).

Questions for Discussion on PowerThirst

a. In what ways does the Rich Young Ruler personify powerthirst?

b.   With all that the Rich Young Ruler had going for him, the mere fact that he even approached Jesus reveals a deficiency in his life. What might this deficiency have been? What does his story reveal about the deceptive nature of powerthirsting?

c.   How can the Rich Young Ruler's story help others to learn that wealth and power alone do not equal success?

d.   Think of a rich and powerful person you know who is perceived as "having it all," yet his or her life is unfulfilled. Where are the deficiencies in his/her life?

3. People Pleasing

This is a lifestyle of doing for others and never doing anything for one self. People pleasers have a deep-seated and unhealthy desire to be loved, wanted, and needed by the real people around them. People pleasers are trapped. They get no joy out of their service, but they continue to drive themselves because they are afraid that if they say no, that the person or group making the request "won't like me."

The church is full of people pleasers who work incessantly in the name of Christian service. The problem is, people pleasers often neglect spouses and children in order to be well-liked by someone whose approval they feel they need.

Before his conversion, the apostle Paul could have been found guilty of people pleasing. He worked tirelessly persecuting Christians. Paul worked to please the Roman government. To Rome, however, Paul was dispensable. His self-esteem was wrapped up in the fact he was a citizen of Rome.

Perhaps Paul was, in some regard, like former Alabama governor George Wallace—taking a harsh position on segregation because of its popular appeal. Some years later, Wallace would admit that the opinions he expressed about blacks and segregation were fueled primarily by his desire to be elected. It also could be that Paul's persecution of Christians was based more on his desire to maintain his standing among the Romans than a distaste for followers of Christ.

Questions for Discussion on People Pleasing

a. In what ways can people pleasers be dangerous to the common good?

b. Why do people tend to grow comfortable with people pleasers because of a desire to get their own agenda accomplished?

c. Think about the people pleasers you know in the church. What do you think may be their motives for the things that they do?

d. Do you think God is pleased with the service given by people pleasers?

— CHAPTER FOUR —

When Religion Gets Sick

Then the angel said to him, "Put on your clothes and sandals." And Peter did so. "Wrap your cloak around you and follow me," the angel told him. (Acts 12:8, NIV)

• • • • • •

Paul then stood up in the meeting of the Areopagus and said: "People of Athens! I see that in every way you are very religious. For as I walked around and looked carefully at your objects of worship, I even found an altar with this inscription: to an unknown god. So you are ignorant of the very thing you worship—and this is what I am going to proclaim to you. (Acts 17:22-23, NIV)

When Paul called the Athenians "very religious," it was not intended to be a compliment. Paul felt their religion was harmful, even toxic. The Athenians had created many gods whom they controlled and manipulated to justify their own indulgences. Thus, the god of war was created to justify episodes of violence and conquest. Mammon, the god of money, was used to justify their excessive materialism. Bacchus, the god of strong drink, was used to justify their drunken stupors. Aphrodite, the god of sensuality was used to justify their sexual orgies. And, just in case they had omitted a god, they had erected a statue, "to the unknown god."

Paul told the Athenians, "You are very religious" as a note of sarcasm and criticism. Whenever the word religion is used, we should never assume that something good and healthy is being referenced. Religion is a very ambiguous term. Much like the word love, the word religion can be used to camouflage feelings and behaviors that are toxic.

There are indeed times, as in the case of the Athenians, when religion can get sick. Religion can become fanaticism and fantasy, hiding compulsive behaviors and delusions and creating a web of confusion that is difficult to untangle. We do not honor God by circumventing reality.

In the book *Toxic Faith* (Thomas Nelson Publishers, 1991), authors Stephen Arterburn and Jack Felton list twenty-one beliefs that constitute toxic faith, including beliefs such as:

- "God's love and favor depends on my behavior."

- "Christians have instant peace during times of tragedy."

- "If I have faith, God will heal me or the person for whom I am praying."

- "Ministers are superhuman, immune to all temptations."

- "Material blessings are a sign of spiritual strength."

- "The more money I give to God, the more money God will give to me."

- "I can work my way into heaven."

- "Problems in my life result from some particular sin."

- "I must not stop meeting others' needs."

- "True faith means waiting for God to help me and doing nothing until God comes."

- "If it's not in the Bible, it isn't relevant."

- "God will find me a perfect mate."

- "Everything that happens to me is good."

- "Christ was merely a great teacher."

- "God is too big to care about me."

- "More than anything else, God wants me to be happy."

- "I can become God."

Toxic Beliefs

Faith becomes toxic when it becomes a means to avoid reality or when it hinders the natural functions of life. As believers, we live in both the natural and the supernatural realities. Neither of the two realities cancels the other.

Naturalism is that which happens on its own, through cause and effect, without supernatural intervention. Supernaturalism is that which happens through the direct intervention of God. The goal of Christian naturalism and Christian supernaturalism is the accomplishment of God's will on earth. It is wrong for Christians to live exclusively in either realm. Whenever we do, our faith becomes toxic and our religion becomes sick.

Perhaps those who live in the supernatural realm are more readily identified as having a toxic faith. Attempts to avoid reality and expectations for God to work miracles at one's beckon call are the signs of a person with toxic faith.

Many who live exclusively in the realm of the natural also may be exhibiting toxic faith, however. If the supernatural seeks to avoid reality, the naturalist acts as though naturalism is the only reality.

People in the Western world who are products of science and technology are more prone to embrace naturalism. In the early 20th century, theologian Rudolph Bultmann called for the demythologizing of the Bible. Bultmann argued that the miracles and world view of the Bible are mythological and, therefore, unacceptable to the modern mind.

Fundamentalists of that same era would argue that the supernatural events of the Bible did happen; however, they would further assert that God no longer operates in a supernatural way.

Fundamentalists believe that the age of supernatural intervention ended with the close of the first century. The text referenced for this assertion is 1 Corinthians 13:8-10, where Paul speaks of supernatural things ceasing when that which is perfect has come. For the naturalist-fundamentalist, that which is perfect refers to the completion of the New Testament. According to their understanding, all that abides today is faith, hope and love.

Supernaturalists would counter naturalist-fundamentalists by saying "that which is perfect" does not refer to the close of the canon but the Second Coming of Christ. The key phrase, say the supernaturalists, is "face to face," found in verse 12. Face to face is an Old Testament idiomatic expression used for seeing God (Genesis 32:30, Exodus 33:11, Deuteronomy 34:10, Judges 6:22, Ezekiel 20:35).

The danger of exclusive naturalism is that it robs the Church of the vitality that comes with belief in spiritual gifts. One of the keys to the vitality of the Church is the empowerment of the laity through gift discovery. Naturalism limits the gifts in the body of Christ to those that are empirical.

Perhaps the greatest problem with exclusive naturalism is that it promotes a form of cultural chauvinism by the West. Naturalism is an exclusive product of western European thinking. The West, which has put its faith in science and reason, has made little, if any, room for supernatural activity. The Western mind looks with suspicion at phenomena such as glossolalia, supernatural healing, or demon possession. Those ministers who teach and preach it are often looked upon with great skepticism.

It is important to remember that skepticism about super-naturalism is a product of Western enlightenment thought. People of other cultures, like Africa, take seriously the supernatural reality.

In the African world view, belief in demons, evil spirits, good spirits, and ancestors is part of their cosmology. Therefore, missionaries who do not take seriously this world view will have problems establishing a rapport with Africans. One of the reasons why the charismatic church is the fastest growing sect on the African continent is that charismatics leave room for supernatural reality.

Put on Your Shoes

Toxic religion is an attempt to live exclusively in either the natural or the supernatural realms. Healthy religion is not an either/or existence in the natural and supernatural realms; rather, it requires a both/and orientation.

Perhaps the words "Put on your shoes," taken from Peter's divine rescue from prison, best sum up what it means to live in both realities. These are words rich with spiritual significance. They represent a timeless principle of how great and marvelous things are brought to pass through divine-human cooperation.

At first glance, the act of putting on shoes does not strike us as being spiritually significant. Putting on shoes is a rather routine and mundane activity. However, it is our refusal to put on our shoes—to perform such a mundane task of life—that short circuits our blessings. So many prayers are never answered, so many dreams are unfulfilled, so much potential is unrealized, so much talent goes untapped, simply because we won't put on our shoes.

The occasion for which these instructions were given occurred during a wave of persecution against the early church, initiated by King Herod Agrippa I (Acts 12). From the initial dawning of the Christian era, the Herod family was among the chief foes and antagonists of the cause of Christ.

It was King Herod the Great who massacred all of the baby boys in Bethlehem in an attempt to eliminate one baby—Jesus. It was his son, King Herod the Tetrarch, who had ordered the beheading of John the Baptist. A third-generation Herod, Herod Agrippa I, had now launched a new wave of persecution against the church in Jerusalem.

The final days of Passover were coming to an end. Passover is that festival that commemorates Jewish independence from Egypt and the establishment of Jewish nationhood. Passover would be the Hebrew equivalent to Independence Day in the United States. Jewish pride and nationalism were beating in every heart. Herod, who was despised and rejected because he was a non-Jew, decided to do something that would boost his ratings in the polls and enhance his popularity among the ranks of Jewish nationalists.

Herod apprehended James the apostle and had him executed. Immediately, Herod's popularity went up in the polls. To gain further political mileage among his Jewish subjects, Herod arrested Peter, put him in a maximum security prison and signed a death warrant calling for Peter's execution the following morning.

What a dilemma for the church! This fledgling young fellowship had to entertain the notion that two of her most prominent leaders would be executed within one week. How could the church face the future when all of its leaders were being systematically eliminated?

When Herod apprehended Peter, he was not content with the ordinary means of detaining him in custody. Herod placed Peter under maximum security and issued four squads of soldiers to guard him. Each squad had four guards. Each squad guarded Peter on four rotating shifts during the night, each shift lasting four hours.

Peter was chained between two guards. Two guards were at the door as sentries, guarding the guards that were guarding Peter. As a final security precaution, there was a huge iron gate enclosing the prison fortress.

All this security meant that, humanly speaking, there was no possibility for escape. The term "humanly speaking" must be amplified because things that are humanly impossible are always possible with God. God can never be reduced to human circumstances or made the prisoner of human predicaments. God specializes in things that seem impossible.

The text says that while Peter was asleep, an angel of the Lord came upon him, and a light shined in the darkness of the prison. The angel touched Peter on the side and said, "Put on your shoes." The chains dropped from his wrists. The angel said, "Follow me." When they got to the door where sentries were stationed, the door opened. When they got to the big iron gate, it opened of its own accord. When Peter was standing in the street outside the iron gate, the angel left him. What a jail break!

Now let's slow the action down a bit. First, notice that Peter experienced a miraculous deliverance, but James was killed. In the same chapter, God allowed one apostle to be killed but delivered another.

Two toxic beliefs that were noted previously were the concepts: (1) If you have faith, God will heal you or someone for whom you are praying; (2) A strong faith will protect you from problems and pain.

The death of James dispels these two toxic ideas. James was just as faithful as Peter. God loved James as much as God loved Peter. Nevertheless, James died and Peter was spared.

The church must be careful never to leave people with the impression that faith in God means automatic deliverance. It must also be recognized that God's love does not necessarily equate to God's deliverance. These beliefs leave people to suffer, believing that their circumstances are the result of faithlessness.

In 1968, Martin Luther King Jr. fell victim to a fatal bullet. In 1981, President Ronald Reagan was shot, yet survived his wound. The fact that Dr. King died and Mr. Reagan lived does not mean that God loved Dr. King less than Mr. Reagan. The reason why Peter was delivered and James was killed remains a mystery in the human mind. Why some Christians are spared sickness and tragedy while others are not is a human mystery.

God is capable of giving us peace in all the circumstances of life. The angel struck Peter as he lay sleeping on the night before his scheduled execution. Peter slept, even though he was chained between two guards with no possibility of escape, knowing that his co-laborer had already been beheaded. Stone walls do not a prison make, nor iron bars a cage. Paul said, "The peace of God, which passes all understanding, will keep your mind" (Philippians 4:7).

The angel told Peter to put on his shoes. When Peter did as the angel told him, the chains fell off and the doors and the big iron gate miraculously opened right before him. Certainly every time Peter put his shoes on thereafter, he remembered the angel's instructions.

Some people may ask, "Why didn't the angel just put Peter's shoes on for him? Was such a task beneath one of God's holy messengers?" It was not pride or arrogance that kept the angel from putting on Peter's shoes. On a different occasion, the Master Himself had washed Peter's feet. Surely if it was not beneath Jesus to wash Peter's feet, it would not have been beneath the angel to put on Peter's shoes.

It is not God's way to do for us what we are capable of doing for ourselves. Without a doubt, Peter was in trouble and needed supernatural intervention. Only supernatural intervention could cause chains of bondage to fall off and locked prison doors and gates to come open. Only supernatural intervention could have gotten Peter past those guards without detection.

No matter how much Peter tried, he could not have loosed his chains. Peter could not have provided light for that dark prison. Peter could not have burst open the big iron gate.

There were some natural things, however, that Peter could, and did, do for himself. Peter did not need supernatural assistance to put on his shoes. Toxic faith is any attempt to escape reality or to dodge responsibility. Arterburn and Felton assert that one of the beliefs of toxic religion is passivity. Passivity, in this instance, means waiting for God to help and doing nothing until He does.

Healthy faith is not passive; rather, it participates with God in the process of deliverance. Toxic faith waits for God to do everything. Toxic faith, in the name of waiting on the Lord, rolls over and plays dead. Toxic faith shuts down the brain and refuses to be creative in a crisis.

Toxic faith waits for God to find the believer a job. Healthy faith looks for a job, goes to interviews, makes contacts and submits resumes while awaiting divine guidance on the right job.

Toxic faith waits for God to deliver from sickness. Healthy faith goes to the doctor, takes medication, and sticks to a good program of diet and exercise.

In Peter's escape from prison, two realities are present. The supernatural reality of the angel's visit, and the natural reality of Peter's putting on his shoes. Deliverance came for Peter as a result of a divine-human partnership. The natural and the supernatural cooperated to manifest God's will. Peter needed the angel, but the angel needed Peter, too. God does not waste miracles. For God to do for you what you are capable of doing for yourself would be a wasted miracle, if it could be counted as a miracle at all.

There once was a man who purchased and developed a rundown farm. No one believed it was possible to transform that property into something useful. He worked hard and restored the old barn. He plowed the hard, stubborn earth and planted his crops. The farm was eventually restored to one of the best farms in the county.

A neighbor seeking to minimize what the hardworking man had done said, "It's amazing what God has done." The farmer replied, "You should have seen the farm when God had it by Himself!"

The point of the story is that the farm was developed, not by God alone, nor by the farmer alone, but by human-divine cooperation. It was God's soil, rain and sun. The farmer had to plant and cultivate.

Peter was delivered by the angel, but Peter was also called upon to participate in his own deliverance. The angel provided light to see, the key to unlock the chains, passageway to escape without detection, and opened the prison doors and iron gates. Peter, however, had to put on his own shoes and walk out of the prison from which the angel had set him free. Once Peter was outside the prison, the angel left Peter.

This pattern is not only true in Peter's case, but it is true for all the miracles of the New Testament. Jesus changed water into wine, but Jesus did not fill the pots with water. Jesus raised Jarius' daughter, but He did not give her something to eat. Jesus fed the five thousand, but he did not pass out the bread and fish. Jesus healed the man at the Pool of Betheseda, but He did not pick up his bed for him. Jesus healed nine lepers, but He did not go and tell the priest so they could be readmitted into society. Jesus raised Lazarus from the dead, but he did not roll away the stone.

Many people are living in misery because they refuse to put on their shoes, take up their mats, or roll away the stones that block them from wholeness and vitality. Anyone who wants a job must first put on his/her shoes and walk to job interviews. God will make a way, but God will not knock on the door of a prospective employer or look in the "help wanted" ads. An alcoholic or drug addict who wants deliverance must put on his/her shoes and go to a treatment center or to an Alcoholics Anonymous or Narcotics Anonymous meeting. A person who wants higher education has to put his/her own shoes on. God won't stand in the registration line, go to class, study, take exams, or write papers.

If African Americans want good health, we must put on our shoes. God won't exercise for us, cook or eat nutritionally for us or go to the doctor for us.

If African Americans want a healthy community, we must put on our shoes. God won't support black businesses for us, or create block watch organizations, or vote, or get involved in the community for black people. What God will do, however, is pave the way for us to walk once we have put on our shoes.

Toxic Beliefs Among Clergy
The Myth of the Superpreacher

We members of that elusive group called clergy often appear so calm, confident and courageous from the perspective of the laity. Sunday after Sunday, we mount the pulpit to speak on themes that are beyond our purview to address. Our messages occasionally stir such inspiration among our listeners that, through our voices, people actually hear God's will for their lives. Whenever role models are mentioned, we are usually named among them. Whenever there is a crisis in the community, we are usually called upon to give support and leadership.

In an ideal religious world, our families are lifted up as shining examples of stability. Our marriages are always blissful, and our children are honor students on their way to Morehouse or Spelman College. Whenever there is a family crisis—unemployment, suicide, divorce, racism, depression, incarceration, drug abuse, we are called upon to give guidance and direction.

Omnipotence, omnipresence, omniscience omnicompetence and omnistrength are perceived as our virtues. This is the image of how many ministers are viewed—persons who are not members of the human family, but who are superhuman beings. Such perceptions, as flattering as they may be, are not rooted in reality and can have hazardous effects upon the ministers, their spouses and families, the church, and all other persons participating in the charade.

While the preacher is usually the one most hurt by such unrealistic expectations, ironically, it is often clergy members who are most responsible for keeping the myth alive. The image of the superpastor is fostered, in part, by a need that all ministers have to be held in high esteem. In order for a minister to exercise positive influence among parishioners, the minister must be esteemed as different and unique, if not superior. When a minister loses the savor of uniqueness, that minister is good for nothing but to be trodden by the feet of ordinary persons, otherwise known as laity. The preacher projects him/herself as having everything together when, in fact, underneath the thin veneer of spiritual authority is a frightened, insecure, lonely person crying out for help.

The apostle Paul taught that the pastor must have his/her family in subjection; otherwise, how can that pastor give direction to the church? Paul recognized the relationship between the ethics of the preacher and the ability of the preacher to be heard. The modern preacher is often guilty of overshooting the target and presenting him/herself to the church as "superpreacher." In order to get a more honest appraisal of the mythological superpreacher, we need to ask the question: Who is the African American preacher?

The answer to this question varies depending on whom you ask. The eminent historian and sociologist, W.E.B. Dubois said that the African American preacher is the most unique personality developed by black folks on American soil. Truly, there is some merit to Dubois' high regard for African American preachers. The development of the African American community would have been greatly hindered had it not been for the invaluable role of African American clergy in the ongoing black struggle for liberation and empowerment.

Much of the black community's social, moral, educational and political leadership has come from the ranks of the black clergy. Well-known and little-known black clergy alike have rendered sacrificial service in the African American quest for liberation.

In striking contrast to Dubois' positive characterization of the African American preacher are a plethora of other voices who are less complimentary in their assessment of the African American pulpit. Robert Decoy is not alone in his scathing critique of the African American preacher. Other works in print and on the silver screen have helped to reinforce the image, such as Ralph Ellison's *The Invisible Man*, and James Baldwin's *The Fire Next Time*. In the movies, *Which Way Is Up?*, *Uptown Saturday Night*, *Cotton Comes to Harlem*, *The Blues Brothers* and *The Women of Brewster Place*, the preachers were badly tarnished personalities.

Who is the black preacher? Is the preacher a helper or a hustler? Pimp or prophet? Racketeer or revivalist? Dr. Benjamin E. Mays or Rev. Leave A Little?

In Acts 14, Luke records an incident in the life of Paul and Barnabas that sheds great light on the true identity of ministers and how they are to relate to those whom they serve. Paul and Barnabas had just brought healing to a paralytic man by the gate in Lyconia. The act resulted in the people of Lyconia mistaking Paul and Barnabas for Greek gods. Barnabas they called Zeus and Paul they called Hermes. The Lyconians had brought wreaths and oxen in order to offer sacrifices to Paul and Barnabas. Paul stopped them because he sensed they were being deified. Paul refused to inhale the fumes of veneration. Paul said to the Lyconians, "We are men of like passions, as you." The term "like passions" would include the full range of passions experienced by human beings, including fear, doubt, anger, pride, sexuality and fatigue.

Paul disavowed himself as the source of the paralytic man's healing. Paul saw himself and Barnabas as the channels through which healing came. Being the channel of divine healing is not insignificant, however. Just as a mechanic needs tools to fix a broken car, God needs tools to fix a broken world. Paul and Barnabas served as tools used by God to facilitate divine healing, not the mechanics. Therefore, Paul was quick to correct the Lyconians concerning how he and Barnabas were being misidentified. Misconceptions often lead to misunderstandings. If the Lyconians misconceived the identity of Paul and Barnabas, they would eventually misunderstand what Paul and Barnabas were capable of doing. They would probably misunderstand the true power of God's might because they had attributed too much to these two fallible human beings.

Ministers are people in process, not supernatural creatures endowed with supernatural attributes. Ministers are not emissaries sent from heaven, but people of like passions.

Playing God is a terrible burden. Playing God or having a Messiah complex is one of the minister's greatest forms of deception, to self and others. It is deception because God's job is not vacant. Even if it were, no human being could meet the requirements and qualifications for the job: absolute moral perfection, omniscience and omni-competence are not human virtues.

A prime example of the consequences of veneration is the life of Martin Luther King Jr. After Dr. King had led African Americans in desegregating Montgomery city buses, the black community naively placed on Dr. King the burden of replicating Montgomery across the country. Dr. King, a man of great humility, was quick to recognize his inability to eradicate segregation in America as quickly and as successfully as he had in Montgomery. In actuality, Dr. King did not eradicate segregation in Montgomery. Even after seating on the buses was integrated, Montgomery remained a segregated city.

After Montgomery, people in the black community laid upon Dr. King's shoulders the awesome task of changing America. Wherever he went, Dr. King was expected to erase racism, confront and convert racists, be fearless in the face of hostility, anger-free, indomitable in spirit and omnicompetent in strategy. In death, the persona of Dr. King took on even greater meaning. Holidays, movies, songs, streets, buildings, schools and other well-deserved honors were posthumously bestowed, often veiling the humanity of Dr. King.

Clergy veneration has a number of devastating consequences:

1. **It minimizes the human effort and sacrifices that ministers make in order to serve people.** When churches view the pastor as God, the congregation fails to really appreciate the sacrifice behind the service that is being rendered. After all, it doesn't take real effort for God to preach a sermon. Recognizing that ministers are human helps the congregation to cultivate a genuine appreciation for ministerial accomplishments. For example, recognition of Martin Luther King's humanity helps us to appreciate the courage it took for him to do what he did and the true greatness of his accomplishments.

2. **Clergy deification often causes disillusionment when people discover that their minister is human and imperfect.** After the death of Dr. King, the FBI leaked news to the media of alleged sexual misconduct on his part. Whether or not these allegations are true, since that time many books and articles have been written on the subject.

3. **Clergy deification can hinder group progress by making an individual's message sacrosanct.** The leadership of many pastors is literally put in handcuffs because their churches will not allow a new pastor to take the church beyond where the venerated pastor brought them. This is perhaps the

reason why God not only buried Moses, but buried his grave. God did not want Israel to build a shrine venerating Moses. Instead, God wanted Israel to move forward under the new leadership of Joshua.

4. **Clergy veneration cripples participatory ministry.** If the clergy is deified, that means the laity can be inactive and dysfunctional. The "Let-George-do-it" syndrome becomes the "let-the-pastor-do-it" syndrome; after all, that is why he/she is being paid. The doctrine of the priesthood of all believers emerged out of the 16th century Protestant Reformation. This teaching asserts that all persons are on the same level in Christ. All believers are ministers, having equal access to God, freedom of conscious and freedom to interpret Scripture. Clergy veneration undermines the doctrine of the priesthood of the believer.

5. **Sometimes clergy veneration is just a coverup for laziness on the part of the laity.** Dr. George McCalep, pastor of Greenforest Community Baptist Church in Decatur, Georgia, has described pastoring as being like a man in a circus who is spinning plates on five different sticks. He gets one plate started and goes to the second plate. He gets the second plate started and goes to the third and then to the fourth and then the fifth. When he finally spins the fifth plate, the first plate is slowing down and needs re-spinning. So the man finds himself constantly having to go from one plate to another.The pastor often feels like that—going from one ministry to another, trying to keep them all spinning. Such a mammoth task is achievable for God; however, for a person with human passions, such a task leads to burnout and disillusionment.

6. **Clergy veneration is the major cause of burnout for ministers.** Because the pastor is called upon to spin so many plates, the pastor experiences burnout. Just as Superman was weak to kryptonite, burnout is the kryptonite for the pastor. Burnout is caused by mental, physical and spiritual exhaustion because excessive demands have been made upon one's energy, strength and resources. The apostle Paul said, "We are humans." No one person is capable of fulfilling

the voluminous demands that are often placed upon clergy. This is the reason why statistics show that ministers often lead in divorce, heart attacks and strokes. Playing God has its hazards. Therefore, the minister must prioritize his/her own well-being. In fact the minister must prioritize his/her health above the demands of the congregation—not at the expense of the congregation, but for the benefit of the congregation. What a minister is able to give to a congregation is always based on what the minister has to give.

Your Health Is Important

The apostle Paul, in his farewell address to the Ephesian elders, advised them to "take heed to yourself and the flock over which the Holy Spirit has made you overseer" (Acts 20:28). Notice that Paul told them to watch themselves before they watch the church. Translated, Paul was saying that the minister should first seek his/her own well-being before the well-being of the church.

Financial institutions recognize how important the health of the pastor is to the health of the congregation. Many banking institutions will not loan churches money unless the church is willing to put a "key man" life insurance policy on the pastor. The banks connect the health of the pastor to the progress of the church. Whenever the great Charles Spurgeon rode the train, he always rode in the first class coach. A deacon who disagreed with this practice asked Dr. Spurgeon, "Why don't you ride second class and save the Lord's money?" Spurgeon responded, "I ride first class in order to save the Lord's preacher."

There comes a time when the Church must help save the Lord's preacher. The musings and ministries portions examine strategies to enable the Church to help her ministers. Clergy need help because, like Paul and Barnabas, "We also are human."

— *Musings* —

Answer the following questions on a separate sheet of paper. You may also use these questions to stimulate group discussion. If you are a pastor or a minister, answer these questions as they affect you personally.

1. How is your minister helping to keep alive the myth of the super-preacher?

2. Why do ministers feel the need to keep this myth alive?

3. Why do some congregations need their ministers to be gods?

4. Why do pastors and churches expect ministers to be undercompensated?

5. What should an equitable pastoral compensation package look like and should it compare favorably with other organizational chief executives?

6. If a good retirement program is in place, should there be a mandatory retirement plan for pastors and why?

7. Consider this scenario: the pastor's daughter is pregnant and unmarried. How would this impact the effectiveness of the pastor at your church? Would your pastor still be perceived as a spiritual authority?

8. What can churches do to prevent burnout and enhance ministerial motivation?

9. What steps must ministers take to alleviate the stress of the superhuman demands on his/her time, energy and resources?

10. It has been observed that the church is the only institution that shoots its wounded. How can wounded pastors be helped?

— *Ministries* —

The Pastor's Action Committee (PAC) is a pastor's support group within the congregation with a two-fold purpose:

1.   **Undergird and support the pastor's alliances with friends in whom he/she might confide.** Unlike many pastor's aid committees that are responsible for generating monies for pastoral anniversaries, special days and convention expenses, PAC will assist the pastor and family by providing emotional, psychological and spiritual support. Such persons, therefore, should be trained and sensitive to the unique calling and stresses of pastoral ministry.

2.   **Sensitize the congregation to the importance of supporting and cooperating with pastoral ministries.**

The New Testament makes it very clear that congregations are supposed to support and cooperate with pastoral leadership. The writer of Hebrews makes the following admonition:

> *Obey your leaders and follow their orders. They watch over your souls without resting, since they must give to God an account of their service. If you obey them, they will do their work gladly; if not, they will do it with sadness, and that would be of no help to you. (*Hebrews 13:17, NIV)

The writer employs the use of two verbs that are used in Paul's household codes for domestic behavior. In Ephesians 6:1, Paul advises children to obey their parents. The Greek word obey is *peithesthe*, which means to listen with the intent of obeying. The writer of Hebrews is calling upon the Hebrew Christians to obey or to listen to their leaders with the intent of obeying.

The writer also uses another Greek verb found in the household codes for domestic behavior. Paul advises couples to mutually submit to one another (Ephesians 5:21). The Greek word submission is *hupeikete*, which means the voluntary relinquish-ment of personal rights in favor of another. The writer of Hebrews counsels the church not only to obey spiritual leaders, but also to submit to them.

It is often difficult for African Americans to obey and submit to spiritual leadership. Part of the psychological legacy of slavery that haunts the minds of many African Americans today is our inability to follow and support black leadership. Renown psychologist N'aim Akbar observed that one of the most destructive influences of slavery is a lack of respect for African American leadership.

Akbar has noted that the slaveholders realized that their power and control over the slaves was dependent upon the absence of indigenous leadership among the slaves. Any slave who began to emerge as a natural head, that is, one oriented toward survival of the whole body, was identified early and eliminated, isolated, or ridiculed. In his place was put a leader who had been carefully picked, trained, and tested to stand only for the master's welfare. These unnatural heads were attached to the slave communities. They furthered the cause of the master and frustrated the cause of the slave. The slaves were taught to view with suspicion natural heads that emerged from among themselves. Such heads were identified as "uppity" or "arrogant" and were branded as kind of troublemakers.

The writer of Hebrews is not calling for unconditional obedience and submission. Instead, the writer calls for obedience and submission to spiritual leaders who watch diligently over the congregation as one who must give an account to God. Failure to support and cooperate with spiritual leaders undermines the spiritual life of the church. If the energy of spiritual leaders is drained by minuscule issues, then spiritual leaders have little energy left for the major issue of watching over souls. How many times have pastors been diverted from addressing the pressing issues of church and community because they were putting out brush fires?

PAC should sensitize the church by helping to educate the congregation about the role and work of pastors. This can be done most effectively during the pastor's appreciation celebration. The goal of the pastor's appreciation should not be simply to raise money for the pastor. Rather, the goal should be to heighten the congregation's appreciation for pastoral ministry.

If congregations understood the tremendous stresses and burdens of pastoral ministry, the by-product would be commensurate financial packages, support for the need to have additional ministerial staff, and a refusal to engage the precious time and mental energy of the pastor on the mundane matters of the church.

Therefore, during the pastor's anniversary celebration, the PAC should find ways to enlighten the church. This can be done most effectively through Sunday School. The pastor's anniversary also should be High Attendance Sunday for Sunday School. There should be proper planning and promotion of Sunday School High Attendance Day through media such as radio, community canvasses, flyers, bulletin covers, buttons and commitment forms.

The Sunday School lesson for Pastor's Appreciation should be one specially designed to sensitize the congregation to pastoral ministries. Following is an example of a Sunday School lesson that might be taught during Pastor's Appreciation Sunday:

Overseeing the Flock

Background Scripture

1 Timothy 3:1-7; 1 Corinthians 9:4-14

Opening Activity

Give each member of the class a pencil and a sheet of paper and ask them to create a "want ad" for what they consider to be an ideal pastor. The ad should include qualifications such as experience, education, marital status, and so forth. They should also include desirable personal traits and characteristics. Ask them to place their requirements in order of importance, from most important to least important.

Introduction

Explain why Paul had written this letter to Timothy. Give background information on Timothy as a servant of the Lord.

I.   The Desire to Pastor (1 Timothy 3:1)

Discuss how persons are called into the ministry, specifically the pastorate. Help class members understand that a pastor should: (a) be called by God to this ministry; (b) have a desire to serve in a leadership capacity and (c) have a calling to give pastoral care.

While a person must first receive a call from the Lord, a person must have the ability and desire to perform pastoral duties.

II. Qualifications of Pastor: Relating to the Flock (1 Timothy 3:2-4)

Discuss the qualifications for pastoral ministry as outlined by Paul. Talk about how those qualifications differ from what churches look for today in a pastor. (Before class begins, make a chart that lists the requirements given by Paul. Display the chart as you discuss these verses.) As you discuss these qualifications, encourage class members to share how they believe these characteristics enhance or affect the pastor's ability to lead his/her congregation. Ask members if they think the requirements are realistic or are they too high. Do they expect their pastor to possess all of these qualities? Also discuss the importance of formal theological training for pastoral ministry.

III. Qualifications of Pastor: Consistency (1 Timothy 3:5)

Discuss Paul's parenthetical statement. Can a pastor lead others if his/her home life is troubled? Talk about what should be expected of a pastor's family, realizing that no one person can fully control the actions of another, even those of a spouse or family member. How should the congregation respond to a pastor whose family is in crisis? Who ministers to the pastor and his/her family? How can the congregation minister to the pastor?

IV. Qualifications of Pastor: Spiritual Authority (1 Timothy 3:6)

Discuss why the church should be concerned about the pastor's spiritual maturity and his/her relationship with God. How does this relationship impact the quality of his/her ministry and Christian service?

V. Qualifications of Pastor: Relating to the Community (1 Timothy 3:6)

Discuss the characteristics a person must have to be respected as a pastor. Why is it important for a pastor to have good standing in the community? How does the pastor's relationship with nonmembers affect the church itself?

VI. Making a Living from the Gospel (1 Corinthians 9:4-14)

Paul cautioned the Corinthians not to think that one who preaches the gospel should not be compensated. As this passage is read, discuss the tenets of Paul's argument as to why ministers should be paid, just as other laborers are paid from the field wherein they labor.

Ask the class to share why it is that some people feel ministers should not be compensated well for their qualifications and their work. Why are ministers sometimes held to a different standard? Discuss the fact that God's servants are helped through all of God's people.

Ask for four volunteers to find and then read various passages from Philippians and 1st and 2nd Thessalonians where Paul thanked the congregations for the assistance they gave to him and other full-time Christian servants.

Closing Activity

Ask each class member to review his/her "want ad." Ask for volunteers to read their ads and compare them with the chart of the qualifications given by Paul. Ask them to share whether their criteria for what they desire from a pastor have changed since studying the lesson. Ask each member to share one way that he/she can personally show support for the pastor. Close the class session with a prayer for the pastor and family.

— CHAPTER FIVE —

Opening the African Window

Achieving Cultural Wholeness

"When Daniel learned that the order had been signed, he went home. In an upstairs room of his house there were windows that faced toward Jerusalem. There, just as he had always done, he knelt down at the open windows and prayed to God three times a day." (Daniel 6:10, NIV)

The Parable of Ashanti

The story is told of a prince named Ashanti. This prince was from a royal family that had reigned over one of the world's great empires for centuries. It was Ashanti's people who gave the world mathematics, literature, astronomy, and medicine.

On one occasion, a neighboring nation was in need of an interim regent. The neighboring nations sent for the services of Ashanti. He gladly accepted and, not many days hence, he set out on horseback to the neighboring country. Midway on his journey, Ashanti's horse was startled by the sight of a passing snake. The horse reared in the air, throwing Ashanti to the ground on his head. Ashanti suffered a severe concussion that resulted in a state of amnesia. Ashanti did not know who he was, where he came from, or where he was going.

In a desperate search to discover his identity, Ashanti wandered into a local village. To his misfortune, Ashanti came in contact with men who exploited his misfortune for selfish gain. They conceived a diabolical plot to deceive Ashanti about his true identity.

These partners in evil paid some men to impersonate historians, who told Ashanti that his origin was obscure. What was known about him, however, was that he was a descendent of a race that had made no contributions to world civilization. The vile men hired still others to impersonate psychologists. The psychologists told Ashanti that he was intellectually inferior. Then the evil doers paid some men to impersonate theologians. The theologians told Ashanti that he was a Negro who had been cursed by God to be the hewer of wood and the drawer of water.

Ashanti, not knowing who he was, accepted the impersonators' definitions and behaved accordingly. Ashanti was told that he was from a race of nobodies, so he behaved like a nobody. Ashanti was told that his people never made any contributions to world civilization, so he was never motivated to make any himself. Ashanti was told that he was intellectually inferior, so he never sought to excel academically or to think critically. Ashanti was told that God had cursed him to be a dark hued creature and, therefore, inferior, so Ashanti behaved in an inferior fashion.

The story of Ashanti is more than a parable, it depicts how African Americans have been socialized and miseducated to view themselves. Such anti-self propaganda is the greatest impediment to psychological and sociological development.

Carter G. Woodson wrote in his classic work, *The Miseducation of the Negro*:

> *If you control a person's thinking, you do not have to worry about his actions. When you determine what a person shall think, you do not have to concern yourself about what he will do. If you make a person feel he is inferior, you do not have to compel him to accept an inferior status, for he will seek it. If you make a person feel he is justly an outcast, you do not have to order him to the back door. His very nature will demand one.*

South African liberation fighter Steve Biko said that the most potent weapon in the hands of the oppressor is the mind of the oppressed. Psychologist Wade Nobles echoes that same sentiment when he states, "Power is the ability to define reality and make others accept that definition of reality as if it were their own."

Such statements should remind African Americans of the importance of defining our own realities. In far too many aspects of life, we have been conditioned to view truth, beauty, ethics, and morality through someone else's cultural lens. True liberation is the ability to think and speak for oneself. This is a freedom that African Americans diligently must seek to acquire and preserve.

At the start of the 20th century, W.E.B. DuBois predicted that the problem of the century would be that of the color line. The color line is the line that the majority group developed to maintain power, wealth and control by legally depriving African Americans of equal access to resources, goods, services and opportunities. Everywhere we went there was the color line—in education, employment, voting, housing, and economics.

The color line that DuBois disclosed still exists. Since Dr. DuBois' studies, the color line has moved from public transportation, restaurants and schools, and now exists primarily in the minds of African Americans. This by no means denigrates the reality of racism in America. The color line of prejudice still exists in spite of scores of federal, state and local legislation intended to scourge it. A color line of racism still exists, but it is written with invisible ink.

While acknowledging the reality of a color line, it must also be acknowledged that a pivotal place where the color line exists is in the minds and attitudes of many African Americans. Many African Americans have adopted a psychology of contingency—meaning that African American advancement is contingent upon governmental aid and intervention. Many African Americans could cross that line and excel, but there is a color line in their minds. Far too many of our people don't cross the color line because of low self-esteem and low self-confidence. How many African American youth, overflowing with academic potential, do not cross over into academic excellence because of an absence of self-confidence? Many African American youth are, in fact, guilty of "dumbing down" for fear of being called an "oreo" by other black youth or being accused of "acting white."

The African American community has not taken the continued psychological legacy of slavery seriously. Dr. N'aim Akbur has said, "When the chains were taken from our wrists and ankles, they were not taken from our minds and psyches."

We often approach life with an attitude that, "I can't do it" or "The man is against me," or "No one will help me." So we don't even try! When we do try, because we doubt our capacities, our doubt becomes a self-fulfilling prophecy. We then blame our failures on the continued existence of racism and not on our own defeatist mentality.

A Vision for Black Americans

African Americans have become the wretched of the earth. No one wants the African American race. The Republicans dismiss us and our concerns. The Democrats take us for granted. Many African Americans are not registered to vote, and far too few who are registered actually vote. It must be remembered that in politics, the goal is electability, not moral responsibility. So what are we to do in times like these?

First, in times like these it helps to remember that there always have been times like these. What we are now experiencing is not new to our people and, more importantly, it is not new to God.

The Book of Daniel is an ancient book that mirrors our unsettling times. We all know about Daniel in the lion's den. Daniel was a Jew who had been captured by the invading Babylonians. At the age of 14, Daniel was transported to Babylon. He was rigorously indoctrinated in the ways of the Babylonians so that he might serve their interests.

He was given a Babylonian diet and a Babylonian name "Belteshazzar," which means "Bel is prince." He was introduced to Babylonian gods. This subtle brainwashing was designed to change the way he viewed the world so that he would think like a Babylonian. The king of Babylon appointed 120 governors to supervise the realm. He chose Daniel and two others to supervise the governors. Daniel was chosen to supervise the other two supervisors. It must be remembered that Daniel had advanced in years at the time of his appointment and was in his late eighties or early nineties.

1. Daniel distinguished himself in his competency.

This simply means that Daniel was competent. The *Good News Version* of the Bible says that Daniel was outstanding. This necessitated Daniel becoming bi-cultural. He was a Jew, but he lived in Babylon. He had to master Babylonian culture.

Affirmative Action is on its death bed. When the elevator is broken, you have to take the stairs; but you can still reach your destination. We must focus on our competencies and not rely on set aside programs alone. Notice that the word competent is built from the root word compete. African Americans need to be able to compete in all areas and endeavors.

2. Daniel distinguished himself in his character.

Whenever we are gaining ground, not everyone will celebrate our success. There are two ways to keep up with the Joneses. First, you can work hard to keep up, or you can trip up the Joneses in order to slow them down. Those who felt Daniel was gaining too much ground could not keep up with him, so they sought to trip him up. They searched for corruption in his handling of governmental affairs in order to sabotage his success. There will always be someone trying to sabotage your success.

They monitored his bank accounts, audited his books, and checked his document shredder. They wanted to see if he was misusing the palace post office, writing bad checks, sexually harassing his office staff, or whether was he involved in the Euphrates River Development scandal. But they found nothing on Daniel—no bribes, coverups or scandals. Daniel had distinguished himself in his character.

We have to distinguish ourselves in our character. We know that those who wish to keep us down are going to try to find something on us—stealing, cheating, embezzlement of funds—especially if we are in leadership positions. We are subject to being asked, "Who you are sleeping with?" or "What are you smoking?" Such inquiries have been the downfall of many African Americans—remember former Washington D. C. Mayor Marion Berry and U. S. Congressman Mel Reynolds?

3. Daniel distinguished himself by his convictions.

Daniel had a stubborn commitment to his God. He was a supreme man of prayer. Three times a day he prayed by the same open window. He was following Psalm 55:17. This explains why Daniel, a government bureaucrat, was also a man of competence and character. These two virtues, competence and character, are the consequences of constant communion with God. Prayer can do whatever God can do. And since God can do anything, prayer can do anything. It was through prayer that a Hebrew became a top-ranking bureaucrat in a godless nation.

Daniel prayed in the morning, afternoon, and evening, and nothing preempted his prayer time. Everyone knew never to schedule meetings for Daniel during his scheduled prayer time. He was a busy man with heavy responsibilities, but he was never too busy to pray. People often use "I'm too busy" as an excuse for a weak prayer life. But the truth is that we are too busy not to pray.

Daniel did not allow success to short-circuit his prayer life. Many people, in the midst of so-called material success, believe they have arrived and no longer need God. Now that they have good jobs and two or three cars in the driveway, or now that they have three bathrooms in the house, God is dispensable. We are all too busy not to pray! With all of the decisions, demands, deadlines, and dangers we face on a daily basis, we've got to pray just to make it today.

4. Daniel distinguished himself by his culture.

Daniel was a Jew in the Babylonian king's palace, a person of rank and privilege among the enemies of his people; but he never forgot that he was a Jew. He worked faithfully for the Babylonians, but he identified with the hopes, aims and aspirations of his own people. Daniel was physically displaced in Babylon, but he was psychologically and emotionally rooted in his own culture.

The text says that he was not just praying, but he opened the window and prayed facing Jerusalem. Jerusalem is the capitol of the Jewish world. Jerusalem is the hope of every conscientious Jew. Just like the needle of the compass points north, the heart of the Jew points toward Jerusalem.

Psalm 137 captures the devotion of Daniel and other physically displaced Jews to their native land:

If I forget thee, oh Jerusalem,
let my right hand forget her cunning.
If I do not remember thee,
let my tongue cleave to the roof of my mouth;
if I prefer not Jerusalem above my chief joy.

Daniel opened the window facing Jerusalem because that was where his heart and affections lay. Unlike Asante, in our opening parable, no amount of brainwashing or misinformation could cause Daniel to forget the place of his origin.

It is a fact that every ethnic group in America that has a healthy sense of self points proudly to their homeland or the homeland of their forebears. Jews open the window facing Jerusalem. Arabs open the window facing Mecca. Daniel's fruits were in Babylon, but his roots were in Jerusalem.

Racism is the dogma that espouses that one race has carried progress throughout human history and can alone insure its future progress, according to Ruth Benedict (see *Racism and the Christian Understanding of Man*, by George Kelsey, Charles Scribners' Sons, 1965). Ethnocentrism is the belief in the uniqueness and value of one's own group. Ethnocentrism says that culture should not disappear, but that it should not prevail as the central organizing principle of the Church. Christ is the central organizing principle. Matthew opened the Christian window to Jews. Mark opened the window to the Romans, Luke to the Greek, John to the Hellenists, the Geresene demoniac to Decapolis, and the Samaritan woman to the Samaritans.

Just as Daniel opened his window facing Jerusalem, African Americans should open the window facing Africa. Daniel was not racist, he was ethnocentric. By espousing that African Americans open the African window, I am not advocating a physical return to Africa. Neither am I calling for non-participation in American life. To open the African window is simply to recognize that we are people of African descent. To deny or reject one's sense of origin is to reject and deny oneself.

To open the African window is to get inspiration from the past, to reflect and be encouraged by those courageous and brilliant Africans who made so many contributions to the advancement of world civilization. To open the African window is to know the struggles of Martin Delaney, Sojourner Truth, Harriett Tubman, Imhotep, Nat Turner, Barry Gordy and many others.

Our fruits are in America, but our roots are in Africa. We cannot afford to be ambiguous about this. Time has not bleached Africa from our skin nor our spirits. Time has only bleached our pride for our homeland.

Many African Americans are ashamed of their African heritage. We ask ourselves the question, as did the famed African American poet Countee Cullen in his poem entitled "Heritage:" What is Africa to me? Many decades have passed since Countee Cullen first pondered the question, "What is Africa to me?" For many African Americans, the question is still unsettled. Negative, racist, anti-African propaganda in Western literature, movies, documentaries, and cartoons have made Africa a negative reference point.

The prominent European historian Arnold Toynbee said that "in his study of world civilizations, only the African had not made a contribution to the advance of the world." This sort of thinking is the reason why African studies is omitted from most public school curricula. African Americans graduate from high school knowing more about other peoples than they do about their own African ancestry.

In history class, Eurocentric history leaps from pre-historic time to Greece and Rome, then shifts west to Europe and on to America. Africa is ignored or is only given significance as it relates to the advancement of the western world. That is why in U.S. history and social studies courses and textbooks, the first mention of African people is when they became slaves. This has left many African Americans with the impression that they have no history apart from Europeans and slavery.

Dr. J. Deotis Roberts has noted that this propaganda was so effective that many blacks and whites assumed that slavery was a great improvement over the African situation. It was believed that in the providence of God, slavery had been established both to Christianize and to civilize blacks from Africa (see *Black Theology and Dialogue*, Westminster Press, 1987).

In a largely Eurocentric society, normalcy is established by a middle class model. The more one approximates this model in appearance, values, and behavior, the more normal (read: acceptable) one is considered to be. For example, when African Americans say "good" hair or "pretty" eyes or a "beautiful" complexion, it generally means that the person has features that closely approximate those of Europeans.

Historian Dr. John Henrik Clarke has cited four myths that Europeans have perpetuated about themselves and their relationship to the rest of the world (from the University of Louisville Black Family Conference Lectures, Louisville, Kentucky, 1994):

1. **The world was waiting in darkness for Europeans to bring the light of culture and civilization.** The fact is, Europeans put out more light and destroyed more civilizations and cultures than they ever built.

2. **The European concept of God is the only concept worthy of serious religious attention.**

3. **The European invader and conqueror is a civilizer**. The fact is, conquerors are never benevolent. In nearly all cases, they spread their way of life at the expense of the conquered people.

4. **The European is the discoverer.** This myth postulates that nothing is truly discovered until the European comes in contact with it. For example, there were people in America before Columbus, but the continent was not truly "discovered" until Columbus came.

Dr. Clarke goes further to respond to Countee Cullen's question, "What is Africa to me?" In Clarke's estimation, the question should be expanded to ask, "What is Africa to world civilization?" Africa was not a latecomer, nor was Africa a passive participant in global development.

What is Africa to me? Africa is the cradle of civilization. The Nile River brought civilization down from central Africa in Uganda to Ethiopia and Egypt, the mother of medicine, agriculture, astronomy, epic plays and monotheistic religion.

What is Africa to me? Africa is where Judaism originated. Africa is the place of refuge where Joseph and Mary took Jesus when He was an infant.

Just as Daniel opened the window facing Jerusalem, African Americans will never be whole until we feel comfortable opening the window facing Africa. However, if we still feel uncomfortable opening the window toward Africa, then let us open our suburban windows to languishing inner-city neighborhoods—the places where we grew up. We can open the window toward Watts, East St. Louis, the West End of Louisville, Harlem, Cabrini Green in Chicago, East Detroit, inner city Baltimore, or Atlanta.

If you are too ashamed to pray facing Africa, pray facing the inner city from whence you came. Pray facing Fisk and Tuskegee Universities, or Morehouse, Spelman and Clark colleges. Pray facing black newspapers like the *Louisville Defender*, the *Atlanta Daily World*, and the *Detroit Free Press*. Pray facing black-owned businesses that will do business with us when the majority culture rejects the value of our patronage.

Avoiding the Pitfalls of Conspiracy

The conspirators knew Daniel was competent, a man of character, so they conceived a diabolical plot. Appealing to the king's pride, they said to the king, "We want to issue an edict that anyone who prays to anyone other than you for the next thirty days shall be thrown into the den of lions." When Daniel learned of the plot, he had a decision to make. If he ceased to pray, it would cost him fellowship with God. If he prayed in secret or private, it would cost him his influence or perhaps his self-respect. If he prayed as usual, it could cost him his life. Daniel simply could have closed the window. Daniel could have halted his prayer time for thirty days, but he did not.

The king's law was to be respected. But any law that violates the law of God is *ipso facto*, null and void. It is the duty of all believers to violate the laws of earth that violate the laws of heaven. This is called civil disobedience. Those who practiced civil disobedience include America's founding fathers, slaves, Mohandas Ghandi, Henry Thoreau, Martin Luther, Nelson Mandela, The Confessing Church in Germany, Rosa Parks, and Martin Luther King Jr. This is movement culture.

Daniel was placed in the lions' den for violating the king's edict. He was prepared to die for what he believed was right. The greatness of the God whom Daniel served was about to be made public. When Daniel was thrown into the den, the lions backed up and lay down. Daniel even used one for a pillow and warmed himself by another.

If our religion is to be valuable, it must always be visible. Daniel could have suspended his prayer time for thirty days. He could have prayed silently. He could have prayed in a secluded place or prayed facing Jerusalem with a closed window. But some things cannot be compromised.

The king had not compromised either. But he could not sleep because of his decision. He knew that the following morning the lions would be belching up Daniel. But God had sent a lion-taming angel that allowed Daniel to sing, "All night, all day, the angels watching over me my Lord." And the angels harmonized with him singing in baritone voices, "Oh, yeah."

Lions are symbols of power and ferocity. This story is downplayed, but it is real and relevant. Our pilgrimage as African Americans has been in a lion's den. This is more than a bedtime Bible story. If there is any story that African Americans identify with, it is Daniel in the Lion's Den.

The song asks:

Didn't my Lord deliver Daniel, Daniel, Daniel.
Didn't my Lord deliver Daniel;
Then why not every man.

We identify with this story because it represents our pilgrimage in America. Like Daniel, we have been thrown into the lions' den. We are a den-surviving people: the den of exploitation; the den of dislocation; the den of historical marginalization; the den of the Middle Passage; the den of slavery; the den of segregation; the den of poverty; the den of scapegoating.

— *Musings* —

Consider these questions for personal growth and group discussion.

1. How do you respond to people who say, "Christians should not see color, only people"?

2. In what way is the Black Church still held hostage to negative self-images and how might they be combatted?

3. How can the Black Church open the African window without becoming racist or exclusionary?

4. How can the Black Church celebrate blackness without worshipping it?

5. Daniel did not forget that he was a Jew living in Babylon. Why is it important for African Americans to remember who they are culturally?

6. With all of the threats posed against affirmative action, how can the Church help African Americans to distinguish themselves by their competencies, just as Daniel did in Babylon?

7. Daniel was a man of character. Does character still count?

8. Dr. King dreamed of a society where people are judged by the content of their character, not the color of their skin. How can we strike a balance so that character is stressed without denying the reality of culture?

9. Daniel was a man of conviction. How can the church help African Americans develop values that prioritize conviction over convenience?

10. Daniel experience persecution because of his character, competencies, conviction, and culture. What is the difference between persecution and punishment?

— *Ministries* —

Steps to Afri-sensitizing the Church

Step 1 — Sensitize the Pastor

Christian Afri-sensitizing cannot be infused into the African American church without an africentric pastor. Seldom does an African American minister come to the pastorate with an africentric consciousness. Most seminary curricula are developed by white scholars with white pastors in mind. This necessitates African American pastors independently augmenting their theological training with African-centered studies.

Most major cities have annual African-centered conferences. At these conferences, it is possible to learn more in one week about African and African American history and culture than in three years of seminary training. These conferences feature courses, renowned speakers, and vendors who sell African-centered books, clothing, images, and paraphernalia. Good conferences will sensitize African American pastors as to how the African American church has been a hostage of European culture. For example, such exposure will make pastors aware of the fact that churches are often filled with European religious images, theologies, sacred holidays, and are oblivious to African and African American culture.

It is important to remember that many of these conferences are hostile to historical Christianity because many africentric scholars and students view historical Christianity as a tool of white oppression. However, as Christians, we must help non-Christian africentric thinkers see that the Jesus of the Gospels is not always synonymous with the Jesus of historical Christianity. When a person who is hostile to New Testament Christianity says that Jesus has failed African Americans, we must repeat the words of Adam Clayton Powell: "The real Jesus has not been tried."

For pastors who want to continue independent study, there is a plethora of material available. Many of these books are difficult to find; however, publishers like Third World Press, Inc. and African

American Images, Inc, both based in Chicago, Illinois, are excellent sources for africentric books and materials.

Step 2 — Sensitize the Congregation

K'wame N'kruma, the first president of Ghana, said: "Good leaders go to where the people are and start with what the people know." This was indeed the method of Jesus Christ. He did not give His disciples the advanced lessons of the kingdom until they had first mastered the elementary lessons. The Master said: "Many things I have to say unto you, but you cannot hear them now."

The starting point for most African Americans is with a "Negro consciousness." A Negro is defined as one who has "damaged and confused self-concepts, cultural incompetence, and confused group loyalty." Through the power of the Holy Spirit, however, in every Negro there is a proud African waiting to be born. Therefore, africentric pastors will have to develop non-threatening ways to introduce africentric Christianity to their congregations. Some non-threatening methods may include:

1. The introduction of African-centered religious art.

2. Bible studies that focus on multiculturalism and black presence.

3. Special Sunday School curriculum during the month of February on the role that God has played in African American history and culture.

4. Placement of African American literature and tapes in the church library.

5. Sermons that present biblical teachings from an africentric perspective.

Step 3 — Develop Programs for Advanced Studies and Enlightenment

Once you whet the appetite of African American Christians, there is a hunger for a deeper level of truth, because truth is always liberating. Therefore, the African American church must provide programs for the ongoing study and celebration of what God has done in African American history and culture. This is why the African American church needs an africentric lifestyle ministry. Just as the music department makes the church musically literate and the Christian education department makes the church biblically literate, the mission of the africentric lifestyle ministry is to make the African American congregation ethnically and culturally competent.

Step 4 — Helping Congregations Grapple with Emotional Side-Effects

There will be many emotional side-effects during the process of an emerging African-centered consciousness. Examples might be anger and hostility toward whites and their Negro allies, a desire to withdraw from whites, a tendency to romanticize African history and culture, and an exaggerated self-concept. It is important to remember during these times, however, that people are going through a natural growth stage. The goal of the Africentric Lifestyle Ministry is to give African Americans confidence in who they are as a people to the end that they might participate as people of African descent and as equals in a multicultural society. Keep in mind that their present emotional state will not be their permanent state.

While members or congregations are going through this stage, pastors must defend the right of parishioners to grieve. Just as abused spouses, emotionally injured children, and other victims with damaged psyches must be protected and allowed to go through the healing process, African Americans who have suffered systemic abuse and oppression also must be allowed opportunities for healing.

Therefore, it is critical that we do not misdiagnose hatred for pain. Suffering parishioners, no matter what the cause, must be ministered to by their pastors. They must be offered Jesus in a way that is healing to their damaged emotions. They must be taught that love of self does not mean hating others. They need to be guided to recognize that one cannot truly love others without first loving oneself.

Step 5 — Commitment to Institution Building

The true test of whether a person is an africentric Christian is whether or not the individual is committed to institution building in the African American community. The test lies not in whether a person dons African garb or accessories, but in whether one has a commitment to building strong institutions such as homes, churches, businesses, schools, and communication media in the African American community. These institutions are the life blood and sustaining power of the community. They are also scripturally directed.

In the Bible, we are given the examples of Moses and his commitment to his task...Nehemiah and his allegiance to the work set before him...Esther and her fidelity to the Jewish exiles in Persia...Jesus in His solidarity with the human family.

As it relates to africentric Christianity, we need to emulate these examples. We need to be true to our task of Kingdom and community building. We need to show our allegiance to the work of building institutions in the African American community. We must show solidarity first to the African American family, which will then naturally extend itself to the human family.

— CHAPTER SIX —

Build Your House

Biblically Based Economic Development

The Lord Almighty, the God of Israel, says to all those people whom he allowed Nebuchadnezzar to take away as prisoners from Jerusalem to Babylonia: Build houses and settle down. Plant gardens and eat what you grow in them. Marry and have children. You must increase in numbers and not decrease. Work for the good of the cities where I have made you go as prisoners. Pray to me on their behalf, because if they are prosperous, you will be prosperous too. I, the Lord, the God of Israel, warn you not to let yourselves be deceived by the prophets who live among you or by any others who claim they can predict the future. Do not pay any attention to their dreams. They are telling you lies in my name. I did not send them. I, the Lord Almighty, have spoken. The Lord says, When Babylonia's seventy years are over, I will show my concern for you and keep my promise to bring you back home. (Jeremiah 29:4-10, NIV)

While reading one day, I happened to stumble upon a letter that was written a century ago by an Austrian scholar and theologian named Frederick Von Hugel. In his letter Von Hugel was giving counsel to his niece who was having some difficult days. Von Hugel reminded his niece that there was no way out of her difficult days except to go through them.

He told her that whether she endured her difficult times bitterly or nobly, she still had to live through them. If she lived through them nobly, time would eventually pass, and she would emerge from her difficult days a much better person. On the other hand, if she chose to become bitter, the time was still going to pass, and the experience would diminish her.

Von Hugel concluded his letter with these powerful words, "And remember, my dear, I have come to believe that there is nothing more radically wasteful than sulking through the inevitable."

This was sound advice from someone who was in touch with reality. Von Hugel's letter demonstrates true maturity. Von Hugel told his niece, "Honey, you are facing something you cannot escape; you cannot go around, and you cannot abbreviate. The only way out of it is to live through it. And since you're going to have to go through it anyway, you might as well make the best of it. Learn from it. Grow from it and don't sulk through the inevitable."

Sulking Through the Inevitable

How many times do we sulk through the inevitable? All of us are aging. We can't do anything about that. We don't have the same energy level that we used to. The elasticity in our step is fading. Our broad shoulders are stooping. There is snow on the roof or we are missing a few shingles. There's no use sulking through the inevitable.

There are many inevitabilities in life. A long-held job shuts down. A devoted loved one experiences rejection from the one he/she loves. A teenager commits a foolish act, bringing his parents pain and grief. A young woman decides to marry a man her parents already know is "no good." These are all things that are out of the affected one's control, so as Von Hugel would say, "Quit sulking through the inevitable."

Von Hugel's wise counsel, written a century ago, reminds me of another letter written many centuries ago. It was a letter written by the prophet Jeremiah to his people who had been carried into Babylon as prisoners of war and captives.

The people of God had been carried away. It was around the year 595 B.C. They had been deported, defeated, uprooted, and transported into a foreign land. They had been forced to leave their homes, their institutions, their culture, their temple, and their way of life. It was the saddest day in Hebrew history.

In Babylon, however, there on the banks of the river, a prophet—a radical brother who wore red, black and green—by the name of Hananiah had been going around telling the folks in the 'hood to relax. Brother Hananiah said:

> *Don't worry. And whatever you do, don't put down roots here in Babylon. Don't take out any long term mortgages or plant any slow growing trees because in just a couple of years, brother man, this will be all over. We're going back to the motherland. This captivity thang is not going to be long. Don't cooperate with your oppressor. Don't seek to master Babylonian culture. Instead, keep learning Kswhaili. This exile will be over in a couple of years. Before you know it, we will be back home, a free people. We won't even have to deal with our oppressor in just two years.*

Of course, Hananiah's sermon was a popular message. It was a sermon that built up the hopes of the people with a lot of false promises. It was a sermon that took advantage of one of the greatest impediments to human progress—human gullibility: that is, our tendency to believe what is not true, our fondness for deception and delusion.

Hananiah was a popular preacher. In fact, he was the most popular preacher in town. And the reason why he was so popular was because of his sunny-side-of-the-street optimism. But his sermon, though popular, was a message that was not rooted in reality.

> *When the prophet Jeremiah heard about the preaching of Hananiah, he confronted his counterpart face-to-face. Jeremiah said: Look man, I know you're radical. I know you're a bad, uncompromising brother. But you know that what you are telling the people is not true. I sincerely wish your sermon were true. I wish that our oppression would be over in a couple of years and that we would be returning home. But it's not true, and you know it's not true.*

After Jeremiah had confronted Hananiah, he wrote a letter to the exiles in Babylon—exiles who had happily embraced the message of Hananiah that in two years the period of exile would be over. Jeremiah said:

> *Do not be deceived by Hananiah and the false prophets who come to you with their sunny-side-of-the-street optimism. This exile is not going to be over in two years. The truth is that you are where you are for a very long time. It's going to be more like seventy years before you return home, which means that where you are is where you are going to be.*

The captivity was going to be seventy years. What did seventy years mean to those who were already thirty years old? What did seventy years mean for the twelve-year-olds? What did seventy years mean for those who were already near seventy themselves? Seventy years meant that circumstances were not going to change in their lifetime. It meant the end of a dream of returning home. Babylon was now home!

Jeremiah's advice to the captive community was almost identical to Von Hugle's advice to his niece. Jeremiah said, "Quit sulking through the inevitable and get on with the task of living." Jeremiah's words were: "Build your house. Plant your garden. Let your children date and marry. Take out that 30-year mortgage—you're going to be around long enough to pay for it. Increase and don't diminish. Plant those slow-growing tomatoes. Live your life; if you don't, you won't live. The place where you are is the place you are going to be."

To paraphrase what Von Hugle told his niece, "If you sulk your way through the inevitable, then you will sulk your way through your entire life." If you say, "I'm going to put my life on hold until things get back to the way I planned," you're going to die with your life on hold.

Suffice it to say that Jeremiah's message was a hard pill to swallow. What he told them was not the politically correct thing to say. Jeremiah's words seemed almost treasonous to the ears of the people. These were a captive people, prisoners of war—and prisoners of war only dream of one thing, returning home.

No wonder Jeremiah was one of the most hated prophets in the Bible. If ever there was a man out of step with his own generation, it was Jeremiah. That's why he ended up in a well. He was hated. He was a weeping prophet, a burdened prophet. He had the unpleasant task of telling his people what they did not want to hear.

Pastors don't get a big pay increase if they're preaching like Jeremiah. Pastor's appreciation day won't be a big deal with preaching like Jeremiah's going on. But Jeremiah was not an opportunist. He did not spell his ministry "p-r-o-f-i-t." He spelled it "p-r-o-p-h-e-t." What Jeremiah preached was what the people needed to hear because it was true.

Jeremiah proclaimed what "thus saith the Lord." Preachers do people a disservice by building their hopes with false optimism because false optimism leads to false expectations. When those expectations don't come to pass, we become cynical about life and bitter toward God because we have held God to promises that God never made.

A lot of preaching that comes from our pulpits can give one the impression that all Christians are receiving miracles...that everyone who prays gets well...everyone is getting instant answers to all their prayers...everyone is living good and problem-free...everyone is feeling good, and the whole world is bright and rosy. We all know that's not true. This is shallow religion propagated by quick-fix evangelists.

In this life, there are some things that we will have to live through. They won't change. They won't be abbreviated. We can't go around them; we will have to live through them. Look carefully at what Jeremiah told his audience there in Babylon. He said, "Look, you have to go through this. But as you go through this, here is to be your response. Build there in Babylon your house. Don't decrease, but increase. Seek the welfare of Babylon because your welfare is tied to Babylon. I know you don't like your circumstances, but bloom where you are planted. Learn to adapt by making the best of where you are."

Jeremiah was calling for productivity in Babylon. Hananiah was calling for protest. Jeremiah was saying, "Move from protest to productivity." In other words, "Quit protesting, quit marching, and for goodness' sake, quit talking about Mr. Charlie!"

Jeremiah 29 is one of the most important passages for the Hebrew people. They rank this with the Shema (Deuteronomy 6:4): "Hear O Israel. Yahweh, our God, Yahweh is one." His words in chapter twenty-nine are an instructional piece for the Jewish community. Some rabbis refer to it as a "survival guide" for Jews who are forced to live in hostile environments. These words are so important to Jews that they represent a model of how Jews are to respond in subsequent exiles. Regardless of where Jews find themselves, whether it is Babylon in 595 B.C., or Hitler's Germany from A.D. 1933–1945, or America in A.D. 2000; the Jewish people go back to Jeremiah's words: "Build your house. Plant your garden. Build your families. Don't make your focus protest, but productivity."

Hananiah was among the people with his red, black and green saying, "Burn baby, burn."

Jeremiah was saying, "Build baby, build. Don't be parasites. Get off welfare. Don't be a burden, but become a powerful element in the society where you are. In fact, make yourself so indispensable to society that they cannot manage without you."

Hananiah was a community activist while Jeremiah was a community actionist. An activist's goal is to change society. The actionist's goal is to change self and to become productive. An activist carries a critical message concerning what is wrong with our society. An actionist is aware of the wrongs, but stresses instead the possibilities and opportunities that can be had through that flawed system. The community activist attacks the system. The community actionist learns how to manipulate and maneuver through the system to empower the community. Activists are wedded to a political philosophy. Actionists tend to be apolitical. Activists view racism as the sole impediment to black progress. Actionists acknowledge racism, but are concerned about personal fulfillment and development. Activists tend to be idealists. Actionists tend to be pragmatists. Actionists want to change the constitution of people. Activists are reactive. Actionists are proactive. Activists stress what is wrong. Actionists focus on possibilities in spite of what is wrong.

Now, it does not take much insight to understand why Jeremiah's letter needs to be heard over and over and over again by African Americans. Sometimes we have to come to grips with the fact that some bad situations simply won't change. All of our prayers, petitions and supplications won't remove it or abbreviate it. We can't go around it; we must go through it.

But, to us Jeremiah would say, "Don't sulk through the inevitable; increase and be productive."

And we, as a people, need to hear this. Black women need to hear this. The attractive, successful woman who longs for companionship. Or the mother who is tired of being a single parent. The woman who is tired of confronting both racism and sexism in the workplace. The woman who is weary of a world that tells her she is not a symbol of beauty. What's a woman to do? Don't sulk through the inevitable; be productive. Build your house. Plant your garden. Increase and don't decrease.

Black males need to hear Jeremiah's message, too. Far too many black men have been devastated by the reality of having to live in a racist society. The deck is stacked against the black male. The black man's image has been criminalized by the media and degraded and scapegoated by society.

We see a dismantling of many of the gains of the past. Our government is in the process of dismantling Affirmative Action. Conservative commentators have said that our tax dollars should go for bigger police forces, more and bigger jails, and poison for lethal injections. This kind of thinking is not going to change.

What's a black man to do? They may choose to believe the Hananiahs who say, "Let's migrate back to Africa." It's not going to happen. African Americans are not going back to Africa en masse. You're going to be here. Should black men blame the system? The system does not care about African American men. The system feels that we have been given too much already. So what is a black man to do? Build your house. Plant your garden. Build your families and provide for them. Increase, don't decrease. Seek the welfare of the place where you are.

Jeremiah's message to his contemporaries sounds a lot like what Booker T. Washington said in 1895. Washington's voice was once a powerful voice, but, unfortunately it is now a nearly forgotten voice. At the turn of the century, blacks had no allies anywhere—not in government, not in science, not in education, not even in religion. We were being lynched as frequently as people sang "Dixie."

What did Booker T. tell his contemporaries? He said, "This is what we should do. Don't protest, be productive. Let's build our houses, like Tuskegee Institute (now University). Let's plant our garden (and George Washington Carver started planting gardens). Let us pick up our buckets and brooms where we are. Make yourself indispensable to the society you are in. Don't be a parasite. Don't be a burden on the society. But build where you are."

When the younger Booker T. was a slave, it was his job to stand at the table and swat flies while the master and his family or friends ate. One day, he went home to his mother and complained about doing such menial work.

His mother responded, "What are the men talking about while you stand there?"

He replied, "Well, things like farming, politics, and so forth."

His mother responded, "Son, God put you there to get an education. Swatting flies is just the tuition you have to pay."

Many historians have been unkind to Brother Washington. He's been called an Uncle Tom and an accommodationist. But Booker T. felt that we needed to make ourselves so superlative that we would be indispensable to the society in which we live. Tuskegee did become indispensable to the South by saving the southern economy when the boll weevil was devastating cotton. George Washington Carver came on the Tuskegee scene and made discoveries from the peanut and the sweet potato that revolutionized farming in the South, saving the poor, southern farmer.

Contemporary African Americans and so-called radicals don't like to hear about Booker T. Washington. His voice was too conservative. A few years ago, one of our black leaders sponsored a leadership forum. A big furor developed over whether Minister Louis Farrakhan should have been invited. He was invited, and I believe that was the right decision. We need an inclusive dialogue on our mutual problems. What was disturbing to me, however, was not that Mr. Farrakhan had been invited, but that black conservatives had been omitted. The conservatives don't call themselves African Americans.

They don't even call themselves black. They call themselves Negroes. The African Americans were invited. The blacks were invited. But not the Negroes.

Some younger African Americans may not know who the Negroes are. The Negroes are those people of African descent who say things like, "Quit talking about what the white man's doing to you and get off welfare. Work hard; don't be lazy. Quit watching the talk shows and the soaps and go to work. It's okay to wait tables, and scrub floors. It's okay to address people as 'sir,' and 'ma'am.'"

The Reverend Jesse Jackson was at the forum saying, "We want self-determination. I am somebody!"

Nation of Islam Minister Louis Farrakhan was there saying, "As-Salaam-Alaikum." The Civil Rights coalitions were there singing, "We Shall Overcome." But there were no Negroes.

For many years after the term was no longer popular, the late Reverend E.V. Hill of Los Angeles, California still referred to himself as a Negro. He was a renowned preacher, and anytime he mounted the pulpit, he said, "As Negroes" or "The Negro community" and "Negroes need to do this" or "Negroes need to do that."

One day, the brothers cornered Brother Hill. The Hananiahs said, "E.V., you need to be more politically correct! We're not Negroes, we're Africans in America."

Hill responded, "I have no problem with you calling yourself African American, but I want to be a Negro. It seems to me we were more progressive when we were Negroes. We had our own houses when we were Negroes. We had our own schools and our own businesses. Negroes built schools like Fisk and Meharry universities, but African Americans can hardly keep them open! When we were Negroes, we had newspapers that African Americans let fold. When we were Negroes, children respected senior citizens. But now that you're African Americans, it's poop, poop, poop...Yes! So until you African Americans can build some schools, businesses and get your kids together, I am a Negro!"

The Hebrews went through the Exile, and during those seventy years, guess what? Nobody was protesting because everybody was too busy being productive. They didn't have time for protest.

Instead of protesting, they were learning how to operate a computer; they were learning marketable skills, going to school, and reading books. They were so productive that when the seventy years were over, the Jewish community was so strong that the Babylonians had no choice but to give them power and let them go anywhere they wanted. All of this happened because they did what Jeremiah said. They're still doing it today. While African Americans are protesting, they're building institutions and schools.

Booker T. Washington had to swat flies at the slave master's table. Booker was told by his mother that he was in school and fly-swatting was simply his tuition. We must never permit the grievances of life to overshadow our opportunities. The true test of our blackness is not whether we can be loud, tough, or wear kente cloth (that is made in Taiwan). The true test of our toughness as a race is whether we can finish what we start.

Very often we have been good starters, but poor finishers. However, the true test of whether or not we are a great people is when we can finish something—build something. It's like chopping wood, no matter how many blows you make with the axe, if you don't deliver the first blow and the last blow, then all those in between blows were no good.

— *Musings* —

If a player gets to first base in baseball, that's nice; but that's not the objective. The player must get to home plate!

We've got to finish something in life! No matter what we're going through, God will give us the strength to go through it. That's what the Jews did, and that's what Jesus did.

Suppose Jesus had given up at Gethsemane. Suppose He had said, "I can't go through with it"? His teachings would have been lost. But He didn't; He went on. He went through it all—through the betrayal, through the denial, the rejection, humiliation, degradation, forsakenness, crucifixion, death and burial—He went through it all.

When He came out on the other side, however, He came out as the resurrected Lord, the Morning Star, King of Kings and Lord of Lords, the Light of the World, the True Vine and the Good Shepherd. He came out with all power in His hands.

As those who have chosen to serve Him, we have been given a portion of that power to get through whatever problems we face. In order to affect change in the African American community, black Christians must examine themselves individually to determine what the Church can do collectively.

1. **What is a church economic development corporation and its mission?**

2. **How are church-based economic development corporations structured?** (The procedure may vary from state to state.)

   a. You must incorporate a business. File with the state secretary the name, address and mission of the nonprofit corporation. You need by-laws that tell how the corporation is to be governed. For expediency, retaining the services of a lawyer is advisable.

   b. Apply for a federal tax I.D. number through the Internal Revenue Service. This can be done by dialing their toll-free number. When you call, you are instantly issued a tax I.D. number.

   c. You must complete an application to obtain 501 (c) (3) IRS tax status. The process from application to award may take four to six weeks. You must be prepared to submit a budget for the corporation, articles of incorporation and bylaws approved by your state and tax I.D. number. You must also include a detailed mission statement of why your corporation should receive tax-exempt status from the IRS.

3. **How does an economic development corporation (EDC) benefit the church?**

   a. An EDC fosters economic development in inner city neighborhoods.

b. It provides training in how corporate America operates. Skills can be obtained to create a private corporation or other entrepreneurial venture

c. Because of its separate legal status, it is viewed by banks, foundations and government agencies as beneficial in fostering partnership.

d. It provides an avenue through which members of the church may purchase affordable homes, become members of credit unions, explore avenues of networking, develop equity, enhance financial security, and foster community esteem, pride, and leadership.

e. An EDC provides nontraditional sources for revenue (capital, associations, promotion, etc.).

4. **What are some of the projects that economic development corporations can undertake?**

a. building of homes

b. creation of business through independent entrepreneurship

c. development of financial institutions

d. subsidized housing

e. food and clothing programs

f. job training

g. skill development

5. **Partnerships that can develop with a church-based economic development corporation include:**

a. a local financial institution that will finance, through debt or equity, the vision of the economic development corporation.

b. The city, county, or state has a vested interest in inner city development because in most inner cities there is an abundance of vacant lots that can be given to a church-based, nonprofit organization for redevelopment at little or no cost by the city, county or state. In fact, it will benefit government agencies by taking unproductive properties and placing them back into the tax rolls, thereby reducing the tax burden of that municipality.

c. It reduces unemployment and fosters direct urban renewal. Communities that are engaged in economic development tend to be less crime infested.

— Ministries —

Faith-Based Community Development Corporations

Dr. John M. Perkins defines church-based community development as the church in the community affirming the dignity of the poor and empowering them to meet their own needs.

There are three ways that a church can relate to a community:

1. *As the church in the community.* This is when the church is simply physically *present in* the community because that is where it is physically located. The church in the community does not feel any attachment to the community. In fact, the majority of the congregation may have moved away from the community and only return to the community for worship and other services. The church becomes a commuter congregation to the community in which its buildings are located.

2. *As the church to the community.* This church sees itself as being on a mission *to* the community. The church to the community sees needs in the community and then develops its own programs to meet those needs. The drawback with this approach is that it is paternalistic. Churches with this approach seek to provide for people instead of empowering people to provide for themselves. This model creates what John McKnight calls a provider-client relationship between the church and the community. The community is viewed as

a client of the neighborhood, while the church is seen as the provider of services. This generally helps to facilitate a welfare mentality within the community.

3. *The church with the community.* This model espouses that the church is supposed to be *with* the community. The church enters the life of the community in a relationship of reciprocity. The church not only instructs the community, but the community instructs the church also. The church and community in partnership identify the needs of the community. In addition, the church and community use their collective strengths to resolve the problems in their own community. Faith-based community development always seeks to minister with the community.

This model operates under the premise that the best people to deal with the problem are those most affected by the problem. There is an old Chinese poem that says:

Go to the people
Live among them
Learn from them
Love them
Start with what you know
Build on what they have:
But of the best leaders
When their task is done
The people will remark
"We have done it ourselves."

When a task is completed, the goal is to say, "We, the community, have done it" and not "The church did it." That is why John M. Perkins defines church-based community development as the church *in* the community *affirming* the dignity of the poor and *empowering* them to meet their own needs. The church is best able to do this because not only is the church physically located in the community, but the church is, in most instances, comprised of people from the community. These two factors are essential for church-based community development. The church must not only *be in* the community it serves, but it must be *representative of* the community it serves. That is not to say that the church should not attract members from the entire city or region.

For community development to succeed, it is essential that the church be integrated with a diversity of people with skills and resources that can be used by the poor. John Perkins calls this the three "R's": relocation, reconciliation and redistribution. Relocation means that Christians with resources should be present in order to put their resources in the service of the community. Reconciliation is creating fellowship among people by breaking down racial, ethnic, social and economic barriers. Redistribution is when we put our lives, skills, education and resources at work to empower people in a community of need.

Dr. John McKnight in his book, *The Careless Society*, argues that the professional services industry convinced the community of its own deficiency so that they will always be dependent upon others to provide services. After years of being dependent upon the professional service providers, the people eventually became atrophied and forgot how to provide for themselves. This produces a community of clients instead of co-laborers.

Community development is not a "from top to bottom" development. Rather, it begins at the bottom, the grassroots level, and moves up to the top. It begins with the assumption that distressed people have strengths and capacities that are unused. Through spiritual revival, the client community comes to discover unused strengths and capacities. This makes community development indigenous.

How to Establish a
Community Development Corporation (CDC)

1. **Begin the process to receive 501(c)(3) status.** This will allow you to receive funding from both the public and private sectors.

2. **Get actively involved in local communities, federations, block clubs, neighborhood watch groups, etc. If they do not exist, organize one with the community.**

3. Survey the community about its needs.

4. Publish a newsletter featuring information about the **community:** profiles of courage and success, announcements about community events, and so forth.

5. Invite members of the community to serve on the board of the CDC.

6. **Work with the community to run recreational programs.** Use your community's elementary school gyms on Saturday for recreational activities.

7. Request that the city give your CDC vacant lots and work with local banks to build low-cost, affordable housing in the neighborhood.

— CHAPTER SEVEN —

When the Manna Ceases

Like an eagle that stirs up its nest and hovers over its young, that spreads its wings to catch them and carries them aloft. (Deuteronomy 32:11, NIV)

· · · · · ·

Then the manna ceased on the day after they had eaten the produce of the land; and the children of Israel no longer had manna, but they ate the food of the land of Canaan that year. (Joshua 5:12, NKJV)

And that is what I want to talk about: what to do when the manna ceases. And the manna ceased! It is possible to become so accustomed to the blessings of God that we make the mistake of thinking that they will always be there. We have jobs, and because we have always been employed, there is a temptation to think that those jobs will always be there. When our lives have been characterized with good health, it is easy to take for granted and assume that health will always be ours.

Think about a couple who has celebrated their golden wedding anniversary. For fifty years they have bonded and blended and merged. After fifty years of being together, they know each other so well that they can think each other's thoughts before the other spouse thinks them. They even begin to resemble each other after having spent so much time together. (That's one of the fears of my wife as we grow old together!) But what if, after fifty years of marriage, one of them gets sick and dies?

The surviving spouse with mixed emotions must take his/her beloved to the cemetery. The grieving spouse is filled with feelings of both sadness and foolishness—sadness because the person has lost a beloved companion; foolishness if he/she never made any preparation for living alone.

I'm sure that's how Israel must have felt on that particular morning when they went outside their tents to get their breakfast, but it was not there. Israel had fed on a God-supplied diet of manna that had fallen from the sky for forty consecutive years. When Israel first left Egypt and crossed the Red Sea, forty days into their pilgrimage, it dawned on them that this wilderness they were crossing was utterly inadequate to meet their nutritional needs. They were in the wilderness, and by definition a wilderness is a place not fit for human habitation. There was no Taco Bell, no Kentucky Fried Chicken, and no local soul food restaurant. Starvation seemed imminent, so they cried out to Moses, "Moses did you bring us out here to die? Were there not graves in Egypt? Things were bad in Egypt, but at least we had a place to sleep and three solid meals."

In their hour of extremity, God intervened in miraculous ways! God rained down bread from heaven called manna, which means "unknown" or "What is it?" At first, the Hebrews did not know what the substance was. When I cook at home, that's what my children say "manna"...what is it?" God told Israel, "Since you cannot plant and cultivate in the wilderness, I'll take care of your food needs. I will feed you daily, just take enough manna to supply your daily need."

They were instructed to take two pints of the wafer-like substance per person. Every day the manna came, except on the Sabbath. It didn't come on the Sabbath because God didn't want them working on the holy day. So on the day before the Sabbath, God instructed them to take four pints of manna so that they would have something to eat on the Sabbath.

This procedure went on for forty years uninterrupted. Like Bubba in the movie *Forrest Gump*, who spoke about the many different ways to prepare shrimp, the Israelites found innovative ways to prepare manna. They had grilled manna, manna-on-a-stick, and banana-manna cream pie! They had forty consecutive years of free bread. That breaks down to 22,600 days of God-supplied manna. They did not have to work for it, nor did they have to pay for it. It came unconditionally. Even when they sinned, the manna still came down as scheduled. In spite of their rebellion, in spite of their ingratitude, the manna still fell for forty consecutive years. But one day they crossed the Jordan River and their feet touched Canaan, the land of promise.

Canaan was not like the desert, desolate and barren; it was a land of rich soil and fertile grounds, fruit in every venue, wells of water; they were in the Promised Land. On their first morning in the Promised Land, they woke up to receive their daily supply of manna. But "the manna had ceased." No more manna!

Now it doesn't take much imagination to see the relevance of Israel's experience to our own lives. Sooner or later our manna is going to cease. Something or someone we have been depending on is not going to be there. The manna is going to cease. It may be health! All of a sudden you don't have the same vitality you used to have. The elasticity in your step is gone and broad shoulders begin to stoop and you wonder "Where has my strength gone?" Maybe the manna is a loved one who has always been there for you—that person who had been your light in dark times, your wisdom when you were being foolish, and your strength during times of despondency. But when death takes the person away, your manna ceases.

For some people, manna was a good, secure job. You had been working there for years, but suddenly you were unemployed because of downsizing. Some big corporation bought out the medium-sized company that you had given blood, sweat and tears to help build, but you were left with no manna.

Some people's manna is a government check. The first of every month the mail carrier came. You didn't mind being interrupted from your favorite soap opera because it was the mail carrier and the first of the month. But then the Democrats and Republicans got together, and the manna of welfare ceased.

What are we to do when the manna ceases? Did not Job say that the "Lord gives and the Lord takes away; Blessed be the Name of the Lord" (Job 1:21)? Job said, "I'm going to bless God even when He takes away! He's worthy to be blessed, He is worthy to be praised. We have no problems praising God when we receive a blessing; we just have a problem praising God when He retrieves a blessing. We have problems with saying "Blessed be His name!" when the manna ceases!

There are some important life lessons that we can learn from the ceasing of the manna. The first thing is something about the inevitability of change. Secondly, we need to learn something about the paradox of progress. And finally, we need to know something about the myth of indispensability. That's what we learn when the manna ceases.

The Inevitability of Change

The first truth the ceasing of manna reveals is something about the inevitability of change. After forty years, the Israelites' manna ceased, which meant that they had to make a significant lifestyle change. Nothing causes us to become discombobulated like change! We are neophobic by nature. Our fear of that which is new paralyzes us from making constructive adjustments to change. In the 1970's television show, *All in the Family*, Archie Bunker sat on his piano stool with his wife Edith, singing a lament on change.

Go and get a picture of yourself ten years ago. You will see change. Go and get a box of Aunt Jemima pancake mix. Look at Aunt Jemima carefully. You will discover that Aunt Jemima ain't your mamma no more! She's changed! When I was a boy, Aunt Jemima was full-figured and had a bandanna on her head; but look at her now. She doesn't have a bandanna. She lost fifty pounds, got a perm, blush and eyeliner. She looks like she is ready for the cover of *Essence* magazine instead of the grits box.

When Israel lost its manna, some were resistant to the change and said, "No Lord, we like the old way of God-subsidized manna welfare. Why should we have to work just to get something to eat?" There were some who refused to change with changing times as they just waited for God to send the manna from heaven, just as God had been doing for forty years. They kept waiting and waiting until finally it dawned on them that tomorrow is not going to be yesterday. They discovered that because of the change, they had to readjust to a new era. Instead of just waiting on free manna, they had to go out and get their own bread. No one was going to feed them anymore, so they had to get up, till the ground, gather in the harvest, grind the flour and bake their bread the natural way. God's supernatural providence had come to an end.

Motivation for Change

God never does for us what we can do for ourselves. God doesn't think for us when God has given us a mind to process the effects of change. God doesn't carry us when God has already given us legs to walk through the change. God won't send manna to us when we can cultivate it ourselves.

One of the ways that God changes us is through pain. God has three change agents: we change because we hurt enough that we have to, because we know enough that we want to, or because we have enough that we are able to! If you're an alcoholic and you say, "I'm tired of being drunk, getting arrested for DUI, and having no money," then the pain has intensified to the point that you have become willing to make a change.

Human beings don't like pain, but sometimes pain and suffering provide the greatest motivation to change. Without great motivators like pain, heartache and hardship, often we would not make necessary changes in our lives. This is sometimes how God moves us. We owe a lot of our progress to pain and suffering.

It was only because God said, "No more free bread" that the Israelites were motivated to go back to school and learn skills like farming and manna-making. It is highly doubtful that they would have gone to school to learn how to make manna if God had continued giving it to them. That is why in Deuteronomy 32:11, God said, "I'm going to lead you like an eagle that stirs up the nest."

Whenever an eagle builds a nest, the eagle will build a big nest made of thorns and thistles for the babies. Then the eagle will put a soft carpet of grass over the thorns and thistles to make it comfortable. When the eaglets are hatched, mama eagle provides all the convenience and comforts for her babies to grow right in the nest. The eaglets get to watch a big screen TV while the mama goes to work, gathers worms (manna) and brings it back to the nest. Meanwhile, the little eaglets are just lying there on their grassy beds, receiving worms, and watching talk shows year after year after year. Nothing changes until mama eagle wises up and says, "Hey, wait a minute. You all have wings, you have claws, and you have beaks." Nevertheless, her children resist leaving. And why should the baby eagles leave? They have no motivation to get out of the nest when the mother eagle does everything for them. Therefore, the Bible says the mother eagle begins to "stir up the nest." That means mama eagle moves that grass!

As a result their comfortable bed of grass is pushed back, the thorns begin to stick and prick the comfortable eaglets. They become uncomfortable in the nest and begin to say, "I don't like being here. What are you going to do about it?"

The mama says in response, "It's time for you to move out."

They say, "We are going to get our own nest." Finally, the baby eagles spread their wings and begin to fly. If mama eagle hadn't stirred the nest, flight would never have occurred!

God says, "That's why I stir up your nest!" We never would mature or develop if God didn't stir the nest of our circumstances and allow us to experience discomfort. If circumstances in your life have changed and you begin to ask God, "Lord, why are you letting this happen to me?" that's God stirring up your nest so you can get out of your comfort zone and face the challenge before you squarely. That is why you have got to praise God—even when He stirs up your nest!

The Paradox of Progress

The second lesson we learn from the ceasing of the manna is the paradox of progress. The paradox of progress is a law of life that says with every significant event of life, there will be loss. It is impossible to gain something without losing something simultaneously. Israel lost the manna when she gained the Promised Land. When the Israelites were in Egypt, they had less than enough. While they were in the wilderness they had just enough. But in Canaan there was more than enough. There was fruit on every vine, water in every well, and fertility in all the land.

When a baby begins taking his first steps, that is progress. However, because of that progress, the baby no longer will experience his mother carrying him. When a kid gets a job at age fifteen or sixteen, that's progress. But when that teenager begins to earn her own money, mamma and daddy stop giving her money for everything. When a student gets a college degree, that's gain. But then that person has to enter the work force, thus losing the carefree life of a student. When a young adult moves away from home and gets an apartment, he or she gains freedom and independence from parental control, but simultaneously loses the freedom from worry about paying utilities and other bills.

When African Americans rise up and gain equal access and equal opportunity, that's gain. But we simultaneously lose the ability to make excuses as to why we can't do something for ourselves. That is the very reason why some people don't want to gain and make progress—they lose the comfort of the status quo.

The Myth of Indispensability

The Israelites at first believed they couldn't make it without manna. With the exception of Joshua and Caleb, all those who entered Canaan were children of the desert. Manna from heaven was all that they knew. In their minds, manna stood between them and death. They'd had it for so long that they felt, "We can't do without it! We need manna, and we'll die if God stops giving it to us."

God responded to them with, "Yes, you can! You can make it without manna!"

Just look at what they did after they stopped getting manna—they beat Jericho, they defeated Ai, and drove out the Canaanites—all without manna.

When we have God (no matter how poor we may be), we can make it! If we've got God and faith, no matter where we've come from, we can make it! Some of us who have "big-time" jobs, aren't supposed to be where we are because we came from the wrong side of the railroad tracks. Some of us were told that we were unlikely to succeed. Some of us who were raised without a mamma or daddy weren't supposed to make it, but it didn't make a difference because we've trusted the Lord!

When we call on God, things change! God does not work on our timeline, however. As the old song goes, "He may not come when you want Him, but He's right on time!" The manna may cease, but God never fails. When we lose our manna, we have not lost God. As long as God is still in control, manna will come and manna will go, but those who put their trust in God, will continue to prosper, even when the manna ceases.

— *Musings* —

Think on the following questions and answer them honestly.

1. If you could chart your life, what are the most memorable examples of the manna ceasing in your life?

2. What were the emotions you felt when the manna ceased in your life?

3. How did you deal with the manna ceasing? Did you move forward or did you stand still?

4. Magic Johnson contracted the AIDS virus (HIV) in the early 1990's. As a consequence, he could no longer play basketball. Using your faith as a Christian, how would you have helped Magic Johnson make the transition?

5. Any thing or person that becomes indispensable in our lives is an "idol." What idols, if any, do you now have or did you once have in your life?

6. Are some African Americans afraid of the responsibility that comes with progress? What would cause a person to adjust to an uncomfortable lifestyle rather than making a life-altering change?

7. Sometimes it takes painful experiences to make meaningful progress. What progress in your life can you directly attribute to pain?

8. What are some of the economic, social, political and cultural provisions that have ceased in the last twenty-five years in the African American community?

9. What manna do you envision ceasing in your life in the next twenty-five years? Is that manna currently trickling away, and are you trying to prevent its cessation, thus blocking your own growth?

Consider the following ten reasons why human beings must be productive through some form of work:

1. Work is ordained of God. (Genesis 3:19)

2. Work generates the resources necessary to supply our needs and the needs of our families. (Psalms 128:1)

3. Work develops character. (Ecclesiastes 2:10)

4. Work allows us to be generous. (Ephesians 4:28)

5. Work serves as an example to others. (2 Thessalonians 4:11)

6. Work produces self-respect. (Proverbs 22:13)

7. Work develops competency. (Proverbs 22:29)

8. Work produces confidence. (Ecclesiastes 5:18)

9. Work reduces community contempt [i.e., "The Little Red Hen"]. (Jeremiah 31:15; Luke 10:40)

10. Work promotes the common good of the community. (Ecclesiastes 4:9)

— *Ministries* —

Faith-Based Employment Services

This ministry of caring volunteers is designed to help prepare and find employment opportunities for able persons. Faith-Based Employment Services (FBES) is responsible for the coordination of the following tasks:

- Maintain and post current employment opportunities in the city. Information about employment opportunities can be secured from several sources.

- Create a church website or use a current site to post job vacancies. Many, if not most, people have internet access and it is an easy, convenient way to gain information. Enlist one or more members to work and provide this service to post job vacancies in the area.

- Network with businesses throughout the city. The personnel department of area businesses can mail, fax or e-mail position vacancies to be posted in the church.

- Develop a "tip-line" among members. It is important to get members involved in identifying and reporting job opportunities that they know of at their place of employment. In addition, when members see "Help Wanted" signs or hear of job opportunities, they should be encouraged to inform the FBES for purposes of posting. The value of involving members is that such involvement sensitizes them to the plight of those who are unemployed. It also allows members of the Christian family to truly bear one another's burdens.

- The fact that such a service is monitored by the church helps unemployed persons to feel less intimidated in their job searches. Those who are chronically unemployed often feel intimidated and threatened about going to an employment service. The service allows unemployed members to discover employment opportunities in an environment that is encouraging, helpful, familiar and comfortable.

- For the unemployed in the community, the FBES can be an important outreach ministry to the community. The FBES can use the youth of the church to distribute flyers throughout the community to announce all of the services of the FBES.

- Another ministry of FBES can be to develop a certified job readiness course for those who are making the transition into the workplace or who are reentering the workplace after an extended absence. Such persons would include recent graduates, homemakers who wish to re-enter the workforce, and those who have been unemployed for an extensive period of time.

Provide courses on job readiness. As this ministry is being developed in your church, it is important that all church ministries be unapologetically Christian and not merely a humanitarian project. For that reason, a job readiness course should seek to incorporate principles from the Bible on work lessons to be taught.

COURSE 1:   TEN REASONS WHY GOD WANTS US TO WORK

God works!

It supplies our needs.

It develops character.

It allows me to be generous.

It is an example to others.

It produces dignity and self-respect.

It develops competency.

It produces confidence.

It reduces community contempt.

It promotes the common good of the community.

COURSE 2: BELIEVE IN THE GOD WHO BELIEVES IN YOU

The purpose of this course is to build both confidence and self-esteem, both of which are essential for promoting oneself to prospective employers. Self-esteem is the evaluation by which the individual makes and maintains "self." It expresses an attitude of approval or disapproval and indicates the extent to which the individual believes himself to be capable, significant, successful and worthy.

COURSE 3: DRESSING FOR SUCCESS

This course provides participants with general guidelines on the appropriate attire to wear when applying and interviewing for various kinds of employment.

COURSE 4: INTERVIEWING SKILLS

This course helps participants know what to expect during a job interview, including the kinds of questions they will be asked, how to respond to them, as well as what questions are appropriate to ask the interviewer.

COURSE 5: WHAT AN EMPLOYER LOOKS FOR IN AN EMPLOYEE

This course helps participants to understand the characteristics, abilities, and qualities that a prospective employer looks for in a prospective employee.

COURSE 6: HOW TO MOVE TO THE NEXT LEVEL

This course provides participants with general information on career development, life-mapping and goal-setting.

- **Develop a partnership with local businesses.** In Louisville, Kentucky, the Rev. Dr. Charles J. King, Jr., developed an employment program for youth called "Project One." Through this program, King developed a partnership with businesses and corporations throughout Louisville to give at least one job to a young person from a distressed neighborhood. Since its inception, Project One has helped over 3,000 youth find employment.

- **One of the primary ways that youth from distressed neighborhoods become productive is by entering the world**

of work. Gwen Daye Richardson, editor of *Headway* magazine states, "There is a simple formula to upward mobility in America: stay in school and get a good education; take a job, any job, no matter how much it pays as a first step toward employment opportunities; and delay childbearing until marriage. An emphasis on this common sense formula would go a lot further than all the government programs that we can develop over the next twenty years."

- **Develop a church-based business directory.** It is not enough simply to help the distressed discover employment opportunities, we must help African Americans think of themselves as employers. According to Isaiah 61:5, the Messiah would help the oppressed become employers.

- **The church's annual business directory should feature all of the businesses and entrepreneurs in the church.** The directory will also encourage members to think about starting a business, regardless of how modest the business may be. For example: lawn services, home car wash, baby sitting services, catering, printing, résumé writing, letter service, etc.

- **Open a *Ujamaa* Marketplace.** *Ujamaa* means "co-operative economics." It means to build and maintain our own stores, shops and businesses, and to profit from them together. During the Christmas season, African Americans are consumers, but produce few of the goods being consumed. The problem for African Americans is the absence of retail outlets in their own communities. In addition, many upstart businesses cannot afford to rent store space in suburban malls. Therefore, the church can be a facility to allow for black vendors to set up displays and kiosks in a building owned by the church.

- **During summer months, the church can host an out-door vendor fair in the church parking lot.** This flea market type event is a means to giving African American vendors exposure to consumers who otherwise to would not know about their products. Church members should be encouraged to trade with these vendors. The cost for the vendor should be nominal. The proceeds from the market place should not be retained by the church but should be redirected toward the support of a mission project in the black community.

• **Every year, St. Stephen Church has a Happy Birthday, Jesus offering collected each December to support homeless shelters and drug recovery missions in the community.** The monies from the Happy Birthday Jesus offering and the *Ujamaa* Marketplace enable the church to promote self-help, black entrepreneurship, the retention of the black dollar in the black community and missions to those in need.

• **Offer GED/Adult Basic Education Courses.** Part of the crisis of employment in the African American community is the elimination of good paying manufacturing jobs. Increasingly, our nation is comprised of businesses that provide services, not goods. The jobs that are available are either high-paying professional jobs that require training and education or low level service jobs with little growth potential. Therefore, continued education is essential. The journey of a thousand miles begins with the first step! For many, the first step is the acquisition of the general equivalency diploma (GED) for the completion of high school.

How to Establish GED Classes

• Meet with your local school system.

• Provide space in the church.

• Recruit certified teachers, support help, and materials.

• Provide scholarships for tuition.

• Advertise!

Conduct Quarterly Job Fairs

• Notify employers of the job fair.

- Charge a nominal fee to participating employers.

- Advertise—monies from the fee can be used to defray costs.

- Create a tracking system to monitor participation and the number of persons who actually are employed as a result of the job fair.

— CHAPTER EIGHT —

From Disgrace to Dignity

The Sovereign Lord has filled me with his Spirit. He has chosen me and sent me To bring good news to the poor, To heal the broken-hearted, To announce release to captives And freedom to those in prison. He has sent me to proclaim That the time has come When the Lord will save his people And defeat their enemies. He has sent me to comfort all who mourn, To give to those who mourn in Zion Joy and gladness instead of grief, A song of praise instead of sorrow. They will be like trees That the Lord himself has planted. They will all do what is right, And God will be praised for what he has done. They will rebuild cities that have long been in ruins. My people, foreigners will serve you. They will take care of your flocks And farm your land and tend your vineyards. And you will be known as the priests of the Lord, The servants of our God. You will enjoy the wealth of the nations And be proud that it is yours. Your shame and disgrace are ended. You will live in your own land, And your wealth will be doubled; Your joy will last forever. (Isaiah 61: 1-7, GNT)

• • • • • •

Then Jesus went to Nazareth, where he had been brought up, and on the Sabbath he went as usual to the synagogue. He stood up to read the Scriptures and was handed the book of the prophet Isaiah. He unrolled the scroll and found the place where it is written, "The Spirit of the Lord is upon me, because he has chosen me to bring good news to the poor. He has sent me to proclaim liberty to the captives and recovery of sight to the blind, to set free the oppressed and announce that the time has come when the Lord will save his people." Jesus rolled up the scroll, gave it back to the attendant, and sat down. All the people in the synagogue had their eyes fixed on him, as he said to them, "This passage of scripture has come true today, as you heard it being read." (Luke 4:16-21, GNT)

"Moving from disgrace to dignity!" These words from the pen of the prophet Isaiah are perhaps some of the most significant words contained in the Bible. These words may not be as familiar to some as are other favorite passages like the 23rd Psalm and stories like Daniel in the lions' den. But there are perhaps no verses of Scripture more significant, or more important than those found in Isaiah 61. It is one of those passages one needs to remember because of its significance to the Christian faith. It is apparent that Jesus deemed Isaiah 61 to be significant. When Jesus inaugurated His great ministry there in His hometown synagogue in Nazareth, He preached His initial sermon. The text Jesus selected, a passage that would be the foundation of His ministry and that would define His mission into the world, was Isaiah 61.

In Luke's account of what took place, Jesus went to the synagogue, as was His custom, and He looked at all these scrolls in the culture of the people of the Bible. The grain leather-bound Bibles we use today were yet to be invented. Jesus read the holy Scriptures—no verses or chapters—that contained the Hebrew words of the prophets. Jesus took the scroll of Isaiah.

The dialogue at the synagogue that day must have gone something like this: "Well Jesus, what scroll do you want?"

Jesus may have responded, "I like the Pentateuch. I like the writings of Moses. I also like the poets—Psalms, Proverbs and Ecclesiastes. And I like the minor prophets, but give me that one scroll, Isaiah!"

Jesus opened the scroll and He began to read. He kept on reading until He got to what we now have in our Bible as Isaiah 61. From there He read: "This word defines me, my mission and my purpose in the world."

If these words were so significant to Jesus, these same words should be significant to those people who claim to be His children. Since Jesus said, "These words are important to me," then we who claim Him as our Lord should adopt these same words as being important and significant to us.

Isaiah 61 was a word of hope that the prophet Isaiah announced to people who were living in disgrace. These exiles had come back to Jerusalem after seventy years of captivity in order to rebuild their community that was now in disarray. They lived in communities of dilapidation and decay. These people—the dregs of society, the poorest of the poor—were trying to rebuild their communities, and they were having a difficult time doing it. They were down, they were exploited, and they were oppressed. They were the wretched of the earth.

But in their disgrace, in their state of poverty and misery, the prophet Isaiah brought good news and said, "Guess what? A Deliverer is coming! A King is coming! A Messiah is coming, and this Messiah is going to bring with Him good news for the poor. He is going to bind the hearts of the brokenhearted. He is going to take those who are in captivity and set them free. He's going to release those who are in prison."

In his proclamation of good news, Isaiah outlined four categories that would be the target of the Deliverer's messianic ministry. First was the poor, those who are destitute and lack the basic necessities of life such as food, clothing and shelter. The Messiah would bring good news for the poor. What is good news for the poor? That the poor really don't have to be poor anymore! Jesus said, "I've got good news for the poor."

The list of those who would receive deliverance grew more intense as Jesus talked about those who would receive salvation. It's one thing to be poor, but Jesus said, "I'm not only going to bring good news to the poor, I'm going to bind up the brokenhearted. Being brokenhearted is worse than being poor. You can be poor and still not brokenhearted. To be brokenhearted means that you are so destitute that it is breaking your heart and you have given up hope.

Isaiah said, "Look, you brokenhearted people, the Messiah is coming and not only is He going to reverse the fortunes of the poor,

He's going to take the tattered pieces of the brokenhearted and put them back together again."

If that help for the poor and brokenhearted was not enough, Jesus announced a third group and said, "I'm going to bring release to the captives." The captives are persons who have unmanageable habits, and they are in bondage to those habits. In contemporary nomenclature, a captive is someone who is addicted to crack, addicted to cocaine, to alcohol—anyone whose addiction is making them dysfunctional. The Messiah said, "Hey, you in captivity, you who are blowing your brains out with coke and crack and alcohol. I'm going to come and bring release to the captives."

The fourth group Jesus mentioned is worse off than the poor, worse off than the brokenhearted, and worse off than the captives—the prisoners. The prisoners are those who have been discarded by society, those who society says are hopeless. Prisoners are those who have been told, "We can't do anything with you! You are so pathetic and pitiful that we've just got to lock you up!"

Isaiah prophesied that when the Messiah came, He would bring good news to the downtrodden. In Luke 4:16, Jesus said, "This is what I've come to do." Most Bible scholars would agree that Jesus announced what is called Jubilee. Leviticus 25 tells about a Jewish festival that was held every fifty years. Jubilee and Jubl mean "ram horn." Every fifty years, a priest would get a ram's horn. The ram's horn was to be blown every seven years and the Jews would celebrate the Sabbatical year. Seven times seven equals 49, after another year they would blow the Jubl, the horn. Blowing the horn symbolized Jubilee. Something was supposed to happen in society—social restructuring. Those who were poor were to gain power. Those who were in debt were to have their debts canceled. Those who lost property were to have their property restored. Those in captivity were to be set free. Prisoners were to be paroled or pardoned. Jubilee symbolized a total restructuring of society; there would be no permanent underclass in society.

Jesus had an immense agenda: He was going to bring good news to the poor. Jesus was going to bind up the brokenhearted, set captives free and release the prisoners. In other words, He was going to lift up the disgraced from their low estate and to a position of dignity. But if He was going to do it, the question is, "How was He going to do it?"

Another question to ponder is "If that is what Jesus intended to do, and we are His body and His Church, is it not our responsibility as a church to target our ministries toward the same people that Jesus targeted?" What I'm imploring is that the church is not supposed to be a country club! The church is a ministry, if we, Jesus' followers, are really going to be faithful to Him. Our official church position should be to minister with the intention of raising from disgrace to dignity the same group that Jesus had in mind. The question is "How do Christians help the poor, the addicted, the prison population, and the brokenhearted?"

We do it the same way John Perkins (see *Restoring At-Risk Communities*, Baker Books, 1995) observed that Jesus did it with three "r" words: relocation, reconciliation and redistribution. That is how He lifts people up.

Relocation

Jesus lifted people up through relocation because He relocated. Jesus came from heaven and relocated right next door to the poor and to the brokenhearted, to the captives and to the prisoners. Jesus literally moved next door to them into the 'hood. It's not that Jesus had anything against people who live in nice houses, but Jesus did not live in the suburbs. He moved to the 'hood where He was born between animals and crucified between thieves, but got up between angels! Jesus rubbed shoulders with prostitutes. He was showing up at crack houses. In fact, He got in trouble with the church folk who said, "What's He always doing, going around whores and prostitutes and dirty folk?"

Jesus looked at those righteous folk and said, "Don't you know that it's not those who are well who need a physician, but those who are sick?" Jesus went among the people. So that means in order to help people, we first have to be near them. There was a time when all black folks lived in the same community because of segregation. But after open housing laws were passed, the professional black folks who lived in the 'hood moved out and left the poor behind. When they moved, they also left behind the brokenhearted and the captives. What followed was that white liberals began to interact only with professional blacks who were not much unlike themselves. Out in suburbia, neither the black nor the white middle class had any encounters with the forgotten, disenfranchised black folks who live in the urban wild.

That is why I believe the historic civil rights organizations are out of touch with the masses of black folks today. These organizations too often represent professional blacks and not the brother who has got his pants down past his underwear. There are two kinds of colored folk, but guess what? Jesus wasn't at the convention of the educated middle class. Jesus was in the 'hood with a different kind of people.

Take, for example, Washington, D.C. You may wonder why there are so many murders in Chocolate City. The reason is because before integration all black folks lived in the same neighborhood. We had stores and businesses there in our neighborhoods. But when open housing happened, professional blacks moved out to a place called Prince George's County over in Maryland. They left the masses of black folks right there in the 'hood without the benefits of the institutions and organizations that aid in the quality of life, such as banks, restaurants, department stores, and the like.

But Jesus said, "Don't worry about it because guess where I'm going to move? I'm going to relocate myself to where the poor live." And, if any congregation claims to be a Messianic church, then as followers of Christ we have a responsibility to the boys in the 'hood—and the girls and the men and the women. This is not to say that everybody in the suburbs has to move to urban black neighborhoods. What I am espousing is that African Americans ought not be so suburbanized that we drive around the 'hood and never come through the 'hood.

Reconciliation

Reconciliation means that not only did Jesus move in the 'hood, He began to interact with other folks in the 'hood. He began to reconcile; He got to know folks. The middle class should rub shoulders with black folks in the 'hood! It is possible to move into the 'hood and still have no contact with the folks who are the 'hood. When middle class people reclaim a neighborhood and displace the poor who live there, it is called "gentrification." The well-to-do can move into a neighborhood with historic architecture and price poor folks out, thereby having no interaction with them.

That's a great challenge for many churches that remain in the heart of the black community. People who join churches like these come from various surrounding communities, bringing with them their gifts and talents. As they join our ranks, we have to be careful that we don't forsake the people who live in those neighborhoods, thus preventing the church members from having any contact with those who live right around the corner from the church.

What is hurting black folks, and poor black folks especially, is not that white folks have moved from them. What's hurting poor black folks is that other black folks have moved away and won't interact with them. The black middle class won't interact with our economically challenged brothers and sisters like we should. We say things like, "Well, they use broken English, they split verbs and they are uncouth. Oh, they're so ghetto!"

Some of us need to be reminded that we used to be one of those people! The only reason we are what we are is that when we were splitting verbs, and when we didn't know how to present ourselves at the Fortune 500 companies, somebody saw us in our despicable states and decided to invest their time in us. There's no such thing as a self-made man or a self-made woman. Somebody has helped each one of us to achieve our successes.

Redistribution

What does the term redistribution mean? I am not advocating that we should take all of our money, and through indiscriminate philanthropy, start passing out dollars to folks who are on crack, who are on cocaine, and who are poor. That would be irresponsible because if a person is messed up and you gave them money in the morning, they'd be broke by night. Christians just can't give folks stuff and call it help or call it ministry. Likewise, people should be careful of folks who always want to give away stuff and always want to see people in the "gimme" line as though they're entitled! Just because someone gives a person something does not mean that it is a sign of friendship.

For example, suppose a fisherman takes a worm to the lake, holds it out, and says, "Here fish!" Just because he is willing to give the worm to the fish does not mean the fisherman is a friend to the fish. Underneath the worm is a hook. Underneath some of these handouts that folks give us is a hook—we can become hooked on handouts.

Redistribution is not giving folks free cheese or a welfare check. Redistribution, from a Christian perspective, means linking the unskilled with the skilled, teaching them and training them as apprentices, thereby empowering them with marketable skills. For example, a barber who has a business cutting hair might see a boy out on the street. The barber can grab that boy and say, "Boy, I want to show you how you can cut hair and become a barber."

A business owner can find somebody to pass his/her skills to, teaching that person what it takes to operate a successful business. Then the person is empowered with the capacity to be economically selfsufficient. As the old saying goes, "Give a fish to a person and that person will eat for a day. Teach a person to fish and that person will eat for a lifetime!"

Unfortunately, there are a whole lot of folks who don't want the poor to be off welfare. A whole lot of folks don't want people to be employed. They are intimidated when poor people become self-sufficient. These people claim to be friends of the poor, yet they want people to remain poor. A reasonable person might want to know why would anyone want people to be poor. Poverty is a major industry in this country, and poor folks are a commodity. Poverty is an industry like computers, automobiles and the stock market. There are in this country poverty pimps who get rich off of the poor. They get rich as long as people stay poor. As long as there is welfare, there will be a welfare industry to profit from the poor. The more welfare recipients there are, the more people have employment. They want people to stay on welfare in order to keep their jobs. It's a bureaucracy.

For example, in order for welfare to continue, there must be not only case workers and social workers, there must also be accountants, attorneys, and program administrators and evaluators. Then there are the independent contractors who provide goods and services to the poor via programs like Section 8. Some politicians get elected because of the poor—either catering to the liberal rhetoric or through campaigning on the need for welfare reform. All of these people are benefitting as long as there are poor people. Therefore, they want the poor to stay down because if they gain self-sufficiency, those people get unemployed. It's the biggest legal trick game there is.

Then there is the civil rights community. They make speeches and write books and make television appearances about poverty. But if the underclass ceases to exist, they can't write any more books or collect any more royalties or honoraria. They won't be invited to appear on *Meet the Press* anymore. So they tell people, "Well, you can't do any better because you're a victim." No child of God can be a victim! Anyone who claims to be a believer has Holy Ghost power, and it's impossible to be a victim with that kind of power behind you. Anyone who can read or has heard the promises contained in God's Word is not a victim!

Now, it is possible for a person to be victimized, but there is a difference between being victimized and being a victim. All black folks have been victimized, but not all black folks are victims of their victimization. What does this mean? It means that a woman who has been raped indeed has been victimized, but she's not necessarily a victim of the rape unless she allows the rape to keep her down.

How do you prevent circumstances from keeping you down? Just look at Oprah! She was victimized, but she didn't let being raped keep her down. She rose above that tragedy and started making money. We also need to hear from Nelson Mandela. They kept him in jail unjustly for twenty-seven years. He was victimized, but he wasn't a victim because he rose above it to become the first president of a free South Africa. There are many people who have been victimized through gossip, ridicule, malice, prejudice or violence. Those who rise above victimization are like the children's inflatable toy that has sand in its base. No matter how many times they are kicked down, they manage to pop back up.

People have long called black folks "nigger." Just as long as we know we are not niggers, but children of God, it doesn't make any difference what other people say about us.

When God Takes Hold

The first three verses of Isaiahn61 talk about what the Messiah is going to do for the underclass. But beginning with verse four, there is a shift in Isaiah's prophecy. He moves from talking about what the Messiah is going to do to talking about what these poor, broken-down folks are going to start doing because God has a hold of their lives. Isaiah prophesied, "And they—the drug addicts, poor folks, brokenhearted folks, and prisoners—will rebuild their own cities. They're going build it up!"

Imagine if Isaiah were prophesying today. He might say, "Those broken-down, disenfranchised folks have so much confidence now that they put their crack pipes down. They've put down their heroin needles, have picked up a hammer and a saw, and started building themselves up! They've started dressing right, got haircuts and stopped committing crimes against their own people. They've started rebuilding their cities. Not only did they do these miraculous things, they've also started their own businesses because the Word says, 'My people, foreigners, will serve you.'"

God wants to take us to a new level. Instead of being employees, we're going to have our own businesses. God wants to give us the ponds where the fish are swimming. God makes us new creatures! God wants to restore our dignity!

— *Musings* —

Answer these questions:

- What does disgrace mean to you?

- What has been the most disgraceful period of your life?

- Have you been able to move from disgrace to dignity? If so, how?

- How do Christians help disgraceful people discover their dignity?

- Why do some people in the community have a vested interest in keeping people in distressful situations?

- What is the difference between being a victim and being victimized?

- In what ways has integration hurt the poor in the black community?

- What are some of the signs that people have moved from disgrace to dignity?

- How did Jesus help people move from disgrace to dignity?

— Ministries —

The Good Samaritan Project

The purpose of the Good Samaritan Project is to discover the resources, gifts, and talents of people in distressed neighborhoods for the purpose of placing them in the service of distressed people. The Samaritan Project is based on the biblical example of the Good Samaritan who used his resources to help a man who had been victimized by robbers and left to die. The Good Samaritan applied the principles of relocation, reconciliation, and redistribution.

The Good Samaritan project is designed to help people discover their gifts and capacities so that they might be used for the good of the community.

Relocation

The Good Samaritan came in proximity to the victimized man. The Good Samaritan Project will seek to recruit persons who are isolated from the poor to go into distressed neighborhoods. One of the obstacles that many people in suburban neighborhoods have is lack of awareness of the problem and lack of contacts with ministries that are adressing the problem. The GSP will seek to build a bridge between people with resources and people of need in the community. First, however, it is essential to identify the needs of the community, which often include housing, education, entrepreneurship, drug rehabilitation, and crime prevention.

To begin a GSP, a survey of the community is needed, as well as the solicitation of the neighborhood council. Once the needs have been identified, recruit people from the community who are willing to serve as volunteers. The era of big government is over; the era of big-hearted Christians must begin.

Reconciliation

Develop relationships of reciprocity with people. The Good Samaritan did not call the 911 emergency number or transfer responsibility for the man to a government agency. He did not leave a check in order to expunge his conscience. Instead, he entered the world of the victimized man. The Good Samaritan Project seeks to inspire Christians to enter the worlds of our those living in blighted communities and those who are hurting.

Redistribution

The Good Samaritan helped restore the victimized man to health. The Good Samaritan did not make him dependent. Rather, he helped the injured man up so that he could move from disgrace to dignity. Redistribution means mentoring persons by helping them discover opportunities and develop their capacities.

— CHAPTER NINE —

The Preacher's Wife

The wife of a man from the company of the prophets cried out to Elisha, "Your servant my husband is dead, and you know that he revered the LORD. But now his creditor is coming to take my two boys as his slaves." Elisha replied to her, "How can I help you? Tell me, what do you have in your house?" Your servant has nothing there at all," she said, "except a little oil." Elisha said, "Go around and ask all your neighbors for empty jars. Don't ask for just a few. Then go inside and shut the door behind you and your sons. Pour oil into all the jars, and as each is filled, put it to one side." She left him and afterward shut the door behind her and her sons. They brought the jars to her and she kept pouring. When all the jars were full, she said to her son, "Bring me another one." But he replied, "There is not a jar left." Then the oil stopped flowing. She went and told the man of God, and he said, "Go, sell the oil and pay your debts. You and your sons can live on what is left." (2 Kings 4:1-7, NIV)

It's a simple story. A woman is married to an aspiring young seminary student. The text describes her husband as being one "of the sons of the prophets." That is the Bible's way of saying that he was in school studying for full-time vocational ministry. He was a student of the prophet Elisha. This woman and her seminarian husband had two sons.

Early one morning she awoke, turned to her husband and said, "Honey, it's time to get up." But there was no response from her husband. She turned to him again, saying, "Honey, it's time to get up." Again, there was no response. She shook him, but he did not respond. Immediately, she dialed 911, but it was too late.

Her husband had died quietly in the night, leaving her not only with the trauma of burying him and raising two sons alone, but also to her complete surprise, her husband left behind bills that had plunged the family into incredible debt. Perhaps it was the stress from the indebtedness that triggered the young preacher's death in the first place. It is a fact that the pressures of indebtedness create stress, as well as mental, physical and emotional fatigue. Stress from massive debt contributes to strokes, heart attack and other physical ailments. What a dilemma this woman faced!

To her credit, she did the best she could. She robbed Peter to pay Paul. She stripped her house of everything and sold it at an auction to liquidate her debt. But the proceeds from the sales were still not enough to pay off all she owed. Her house was empty, her cupboard was bare, there was nothing left, but bill collectors were still knocking at her door, demanding payment. They threatened to take her two sons and sell them as slaves for collateral if the bills were not paid.

What a predicament to be in! But it is a predicament that defines many of us today. Statistics tell us that 25% of the income of an average family in this country is applied to debt retirement, and that figure does not include home mortgages. This is what I refer to as "dumb debt." Dumb debt is when we use credit to purchase items that depreciate in value. A good example of dumb debt is a car loan or a credit card that has an 18 percent interest rate, or department store cards at 19-21 percent interest, even more.

Suppose a person has a credit card with a $3,000 balance at 18 percent interest. Then suppose the cardholder makes a minimum payment, as most people do, of $50 a month. The majority of that minimum payment will go to finance charges so that it would take years to pay off that debt.

Not all debt is dumb, however. When items that appreciate or produce wealth are purchased on credit, such as real estate, or when the value exceeds or equals the amount owed against it, that is smart debt!

The experience of the preacher's wife contains several lessons that can help us. If this lady were on *Oprah*, and Oprah asked her to give advice to the listeners, I think the first thing she would say is, "Don't presume about tomorrow. My husband took out a lot of credit. He presumed that he would earn enough, would have sufficient resources, or would live long enough to pay for them."

The Book of James 4:13-14 reads, "Look here, you people who say, 'today or tomorrow we are going to such and such a town, stay there a year and open up a profitable business.' How do you know what is going to happen tomorrow?"

The second word of advice she probably would give is that husbands and wives together should be partners in financial planning. All decisions should be mutual. Major expenditures must be a joint decision. Both partners must know the financial status of the family. Neither partner can afford to be passive or ignorant of the family's financial status.

Nothing puts a strain on marriage like debt. Fifty-five percent of all marriages that end in divorce do so because of debt. We say "Til death do us part," but we really mean until debt do we part!

The third piece of advice she might give is that people need to be insured. Her husband had no insurance. Granted, he was a prophet, and it must have been hard for prophets to find insurance because of the dangers of declaring, "what thus saith the Lord!" Therefore, his wife was left in debt to fend for herself.

What's in Your House?

This disillusioned woman found Elisha, her husband's mentor and seminary professor. She poured out her heart to him. "Your student, and my husband, is dead! You know he revered God. You know that he was diligent in his preparation. You know of his ambition to serve God. But now, he's dead. Now the creditors are banging at my door demanding payment, or they are going to take my two sons as slaves for collateral!"

Elisha listened as the preacher's wife bare her soul to him. He listened as she described the incredible pressure she was under because of the bills she inherited.

It is no surprise that Elisha listened to her. After all, her late husband was his student. But what is surprising is Elisha's response to this woman's nightmare. He was not quick with sympathy or volunteerism. He was not moved by an overpowering impulse to rescue her from her dilemma. In fact, his response seemed quite indifferent and cold. He sounded like a disciple of Rush Limbaugh. Elisha told her, "What do you want me to do? What's in your house?"

Elisha refused to commiserate with her or to engage in a pity party with her. When she heard Elisha's response, she probably was taken aback. She likely thought, "How can you be so indifferent? You are a man of God!"

But Elisha's response was not at all callous or indifferent; rather, it reflects wisdom as well as the best approach on how to help people. The easiest thing in the world for Elisha would have been to reach in his pocket and give the woman a handout. But by doing this, he would have disabled her. By bailing her out, he would have fostered dependency and a consciousness of victimization, which dwells on how bad a situation appears, looks for handouts and not hand-ups, retreats from personal responsibility, fails to help oneself, and exaggerates the severity of one's condition.

Elisha was trying to empower sufficiency, not enable dependency. Elisha knew that the best person to solve a problem is the person who has the problem. Elisha was trying to make her self-reliant by stirring up creativity that the woman did not know that she possessed.

The widow told Elisha, "I have nothing. My minks are gone. My furniture has been repossessed. The cable and the phone have been disconnected. My jewelry is in the pawn shop. All I have left is a jar of anointing oil."

Herein is a principle of how God performs miracles. God seldom creates something from nothing. God usually takes what a person already has and either uses it or multiplies it. Do you remember when Jesus fed the 5000 (Matthew 14:15-21)? Jesus took a boy's lunch—two fish and five barley loaves—blessed it and multiplied it. Jesus could have called down a complete meal from heaven. Instead, He chose to make more out of something that was already in existence.

Knowing the preacher's wife possessed nothing more than a jar of oil, Elisha told the woman to send her boys into the neighborhood and ask the neighbors for their empty oil barrels. They were instructed to get as many as they could. So, they go over to Ms. Ferguson's house and say, "Mama wants to know if you have any empty oil barrels."

Then they went to Ms. Webster's house: "Mama wants to know, do you have any empty oil barrels?" They went from house to house.

When I was a boy, my mama would send me to the neighbor's house to borrow things when we ran out. I remember going over to Ms. Tinsley's house or Ms. Caldwell's house or Ms. Roberts' house. But, unlike the widow's children, when my mama sent me, she sent me to borrow milk, flour or salt, but never the empty containers!

Can you imagine the gossip that was going through the neighborhood? I am sure the neighbors were saying things like, "You know, that woman hasn't been right ever since her husband died." You can't be afraid of what folk might say when you want God to bless you.

When all the empty barrels had been gathered, the prophet told her to shut the door. Some things God wants to do in our lives are private. When you rejoice because of what God has done and people ask, "What happened?" just tell them, "You don't know like I know what the Lord has done for me!"

The woman took her little oil and poured it from the jar into the barrel—and the oil just kept flowing. She went from barrel to barrel and the oil just kept flowing. The barrels kept filling up until all the barrels were full. Only when they were all full did the oil stop flowing.

Then the prophet told her, "Sell the oil and pay off your bills." We don't know what bills she paid off first. If she was smart, she paid off the high interest rate bills first. Then once a bill was paid, she didn't take the freed up money and go to the mall; she applied the freed up money to the next bill.

God expects us to do the possible and leave the impossible to Him. It was possible for the woman to gather the oil barrels, pour the oil, and sell the oil barrels. But only God could make the oil flow freely. The reason why most Christians are not blessed more is not because of God's frugality or reluctance; it is because of our incapacity to receive.

When did the oil stop flowing? When they ran out of barrels. If only ten barrels were filled, it was because they only had ten barrels. If they had kept on bringing barrels, they would have kept on receiving oil. We have some information on how much God will bless us. Jesus said, "Be it unto you according to your faith."

— *Musings* —

The church is a helping institution, but I do not believe that we help people if we do not help them to do for themselves. Some people get addicted to temporary relief, and temporary relief usually becomes permanent dependence. That's why it is wise to ask people soliciting your aid, "What's in your house?"

Some people have no sense of responsibility and will use their own money for thrills, then borrow your money for bills. Before we can buy thrills, we must take care of our bills. Far too many people prioritize cable television, Lotto tickets, new clothes, the latest $150 athletic shoes for their children, dining out, manicured nails, over paying utilities, food and rent.

There actually are people who get mad at you if you won't finance their thrills. They feel that they are entitled to your money. Ask them, "What's in your house?"

Problems are real. Almost everyone faces a difficult situation at some point in life. Every person who is facing difficulty should ask himself or herself, "What do I have in my house?"

God won't do any more for us than our faith will let Him. Paul said, "Now unto Him who is able to do exceeding abundantly more than you are able to ask or think" (Ephesians 3:20). If your life is stuck and stagnate, it's not because God's isn't ready to bless you; you are not ready to receive. We must move to a point of faith so that we can say, "Any way you bless me Lord, I'll be satisfied!"

— *Ministries* —

Christian Money Management Seminar

1. **Basic Biblical Principles:**

   - God owns everything!

   - Christians are stewards of God's creation, possessions and wealth.

   - God is the Source of all wealth.

   - Contentment through Jesus Christ ... not money!

   - Only God can protect us.

   - Serve God first. Never put mammon or any other god before God!

   - God promises to care for us.

Goal: Be generally familiar with what God says about money, wealth and income. Memorize at least two to three passages on these matters. Underline the ones that most pertain to your life and this present time.

Objective: To assist Christian families in developing an effective, simple and proven Christian money-management/debt reduction plan of action.

Method: To introduce Christians to what the Bible teaches regarding money, income and wealth, and how this can, should, or should not impact our personal relationship with God through a four-week seminar, workshop or Sunday School class.

2. **The Truth about Tithing**

   - What is tithing?

   - Why does God call us to tithe?

   - Where should our tithes go?

   - Who should tithe and who should not tithe?

- How do I tithe?

- What does the tithe do for God? What does the tithe do for the giver?

Goal: Write down (with your spouse, if married) a 20- to 30-word statement on tithing. Share it with your pastor. Keep the statement in an accessible area. Refer to it from time to time.

3. A Basic Christian Financial Planning Process

- Write down personal, family and business/career goals.

- Determine the potential cost in time and money.

- Establish a time line: When are you going to reach said goals?

Goal: Pray, study, and consult. Determine where God wants you to go. Then, start going there! Accept your Christ-centered goal and purpose, regardless of the consequences. Remember Jesus accepted His. The least you can do is accept yours!

4. Steps to Successful Financial Planning

- Write down your income, expenses, debts and assets.

- Determine whether your expenses exceed your income

- Determine whether your debts exceed your assets.

- Determine where you can reduce expenses.

- Determine your total monthly debt payments.

Goal: Reduce your expenses (on paper) until you are living on less than 80 percent of your income. Stop creating more consumer debt, now! Husbands and wives are one flesh. Be totally open, honest and non-judgmental with your financial picture. No more secrets, no more judgments. Remember, marriage is for better or for worse! Single people should be equally honest in their assessment of their financial picture.

Then create a budget. Make sure the first 10 percent goes to God. Write the budget down. Consult a Christian financial counselor. Be accountable to yourself or another party regarding the attainment of your goals. Listen to sound advice. Adopt reasonable suggestions for money management. The Bible urges Christians to seek wise counsel.

5. Reducing Consumer Debt

- Keep in mind that giving more to creditors means giving less to God.

- Search the Scriptures to determine what the Bible says about debt.

- Discuss what the Bible says regarding contentment.

- Imagine living debt free. Could you then give more to God? Could you do more for God?

Goal: Write down every single creditor, address, monthly payment amount and when said amount is due. Total the amount. Break it down into yearly, monthly and weekly amounts. How do you eat an elephant? One bite at a time! See if your Christian financial counselor can assist you in making mutually beneficial arrangements with your creditors. Determine to live debt free and determine to stay debt free! Then, write down all you could do and all you could give to God if you were living debt free.

Basic Biblical Principles on Money, Etc.

Psalm 24: 1-2
Samuel 2:7-10
1 Corinthians 4:2
Matthew 25: 14-30
Proverbs 3:13-17
Philippians 4:11-12
1 Timothy 6:6-10
Jeremiah 9:23-24
1 Timothy 5:17-18
Acts 4: 34-35
Philippians 4:19
Matthew 6:31-34
Proverbs 3:13-14
Proverbs 22:7
1 Timothy 5:8

Proverbs 6:6-11
Deuteronomy 15:7
1 Timothy 6:18-19
1 Corinthians 7:23
1 Chronicles 29: 11-12
Deuteronomy 8:18
2 Peter 4:10
John 14:27
Hebrews 13:5
Matthew 6:24
James 5:1-5
1 Timothy 6:17-19
Acts 2:44-45
2 Corinthians 8:1-2
Hebrews 13:5

Luke 16:11

Proverbs 24:3-4

Deuteronomy 28:43-45

Proverbs 28:20

Proverbs 21:20

Proverbs 3:9-10

Acts 20:35

References for More Information on Christian Financial Planning and Stewardship:

The Real Truth About Tithing, by Mark Barclay

Creating Wealth, by Corbin Seavers

Learn to Earn, by Peter Lynch

Biblically Based Financial Planning, by Daniel L. Hardt

Understanding Financial Stewardship, by Charles Stanley

How to Manage Your Money, by Larry Burkett

— CHAPTER TEN —

The Fate of an Empty Life

When an evil spirit comes out of a man, it goes through arid places seeking rest and does not find it. Then it says, 'I will return to the house I left.' When it arrives, it finds the house unoccupied, swept clean and put in order. Then it goes and takes with it seven other spirits more wicked than itself, and they go in and live there. And the final condition of that man is worse than the first. That is how it will be with this wicked generation. (Matthew 12:43-45, NIV)

One of the richest men of the twentieth century was railroad and steel baron, J. P. Morgan. He, along with millionaire Andrew Carnegie, controlled the entire steel industry in the United States at the beginning of the 20th century. Morgan lived in a fifty-seven room mansion in Glen Cove, New York. His house was a magnificent structure located on a seventy-six acre island. At the turn of the century it was appraised at over one million dollars. It was one of the great show pieces of the nation. It was cared for by a staff of servants. Many of the most elite social affairs of the rich and famous were held at the Glen Cove mansion.

But after J.P. Morgan's death in 1913, the colossal showplace became a white elephant. No one lived in it because no one could afford to buy it and maintain it. With the passing of years, it became unoccupied, unkempt and dilapidated. This persisted for thirty-nine years until the house was sold to the city of Glen Cove for $5,233.00, which represented the back taxes for one year.

Just think of it. A structure that once was the home of one of the richest men in the world, a structure that was once appraised at one million dollars, a facility that at one time was the show piece of the nation had declined in a span of sixty years to the value of a paltry $5,233.00.

This is the fate of many houses, large and small, when they are unoccupied and empty. Dust gathers, plaster falls off the walls, paint chips away, and rodents or other vermin are its sole inhabitants—all the while, the value of the structure continues to spiral downward.

In the little parable about the seven spirits, Jesus conveyed the same sentiment. The fate of an empty life is similar to the fate of an empty house. Jesus said a man chased away an evil spirit from his house that had tormented him for years. In Jesus' day, belief in demons was widespread. The prevalent cosmology assigned God to a realm of calm and tranquility above the sky. Earth was the abode of humanity. In between God's elevated dwelling place and humanity's earthly abode was the demon-filled air. Humankind's most feared opponent was the demon-possessed air. The ancients believed that the air was literally infested with unseen spirit-forces of evil. Paul warned the Christians in Ephesus about the "prince of the power of the air" (Ephesians 2:2).

These evil spirits were believed to invade a person's life, bringing them mental, psychological and physical problems. The man in Jesus' parable had been tormented by one of these demonic forces. One day, after being totally exasperated with the evil spirit, the man decided to do something about it. The man did some house cleaning. He swept the rooms and cleaned up the house from the cellar to the attic. The demon was expelled and rejoined the other spirits of the air.

For the first time in a long time, the man was experiencing peace. He was no longer disturbed with depressing thoughts and disheartening emotions. The evil spirit had been banished. However, the man's freedom from demonic torture was not long-lasting. Practically before he realized it, a plague of other evil spirits came upon him, creating a situation worse than before. The banished demon came back, peeped in to see who had moved into his former residence and saw nothing but bare walls and emptiness. The evil spirit moved in again and brought with him seven of his cronies, each with ten servants and a chauffeur! Jesus says the man's latter state was much worse than his former.

It is hard for us to relate to this parable because we are people of science and knowledge. We think that demons don't exist. We are too sophisticated to believe in the reality of evil spirits. We know that if there is evil in the world, there is some natural cause to explain it. We accept realities that are empirically based and scientifically verifiable. Our analysis of personal evils are rationally understood through the insights of Freudian and Jungian psychology. The crises that plague our cities—black on black crime, drug abuse, the devaluation of human life, and the disrespect for authority are not attributed to demonic activity. No one in this post-modern world talks about the demonic. You won't hear about it on *Crossfire* or CNN, and you won't read about it in *Time* or *Newsweek*.

We solve our social and economic problems through politics. We solve our legal problems through the judicial system. We solve our personal disagreements through arguments, and our international dissension through war. There is no room for prayer. If there is a summit on black on black violence, the guest list includes criminologists, civil rights activists, sociologists, psychologists, politicians and educators. Conspicuously absent will be the church people who are willing to trace the pathologies to the activity of demonic forces.

Let me make it clear that I believe in the reality of demonic forces. But I also know that God has given us a name through which we can take authority over the power of the demons—by the Name of Jesus. I am not talking about hocus pocus. The name of Jesus is not a magical incantation. What is important in the name of Jesus is the authority of that name. An American ambassador to a foreign country speaks in the name of the President of the United States. A police officer knocks on a door and says, "Open up in the name of the law!" A name can carry authority.

Jesus invites His people to use His name. He transfers divine authority to us through His name. Power is enshrined in His name. That's why Jesus guaranteed so much to believers in His name. Listen to Jesus:

> *And whoso shall receive one such little child in my name re-ceiveth me.* (Matthew 18:5, KJV)

For where two or three are gathered together in my name, there am I in the midst of them. (Matthew 18:20, KJV)

And Jesus answered and said, Verily I say unto you, There is no man that hath left house, or brethren, or sisters, or father, or mother, or wife, or children, or lands, for my sake, and the gospel's, But he shall receive an hundredfold now in this time, houses, and brethren, and sisters, and mothers, and children, and lands, with persecutions; and in the world to come eternal life. (Mark 10:29-30, KJV)

For whosoever shall give you a cup of water to drink in my name, because ye belong to Christ, verily I say unto you, he shall not lose his reward. (Mark 9:41, KJV)

And these signs shall follow them that believe; In my name shall they cast out devils; they shall speak with new tongues. (Mark 16:17, KJV)

And whatsoever ye shall ask in my name, that will I do, that the Father may be glorified in the Son. (John 14:13, KJV)

Dr. William A. Jones, pastor of Bethany Baptist Church in Brooklyn, New York has said that all the young church had was the name of Jesus. They had no money, no property, no political clout, no civic influence, and no social standing. But His name was enough! Peter preached in His name on the day of Pentecost and 3,000 souls were added to the church. Peter and John met a lame man outside the beautiful gate of the Temple (Acts 3:2). The man was begging for alms. But Peter said, "Silver and gold have I none but what I do have, I give unto you. In the name of Jesus stand up and walk."

The name of Jesus is an awesome weapon for the believer. But caution is needed. In Acts 19, we are told of the seven sons of Sceva who tried to cast out a demon in the name of Jesus, but the evil spirit knew they were phonies and chased them and beat them up. No one can use the name of Jesus unless that person confesses Jesus as Lord.

But for those who don't believe in the demonic, there are still some great lessons to be learned from this story of the empty house.

If you are trying to expel something from your life—depression, grief, worry, hate, habits, drugs, alcohol, or destructive relationships, Jesus is the answer. If you are trying to banish, eject and permanently drive out that which torments you, Jesus gives the prescription.

The Persistence of Evil

What we can learn from this, first of all, is that evil is persistent. He drove out the evil, but the evil came back. When we get rid of one problem, we need not think that it won't try to come back. Overcome one bad habit, and we can't afford to think that it won't try to come back.

Those who have driven drug and alcohol habits from their lives know that each victory is just one day at a time. One drink is too many and a thousand drinks are not enough! Every problem that we expel from our lives is looking for an opportunity to come back. We kick one problem out the front door, and here comes another problem sneaking in through the back door. You kick lust out the front door, and here comes pride and greed through the window. The struggle against evil is a lifelong conflict.

African Americans fought and died to get rid of Jim Crow, segregation, and Ku Klux Klan terrorism. Once these evil menaces were eradicated, along came drugs, black on black crime, and a plethora of social problems. Evil is persistent!

Not only does this parable teach us that evil is persistent, but it also teaches us that one cannot build a positive life on negative expulsions. A Christian life cannot be built on "no's" and "not's," or "do's" and "don'ts." This man expelled an evil spirit and that is all that he did. He did not go beyond the negative expulsion of evil to embracing the positive affirmation of something good. This man got rid of some evil, some bad habit, but he didn't adopt a new and better interest. He cleaned the house, but he left the house empty; and an empty house or an empty life always invites undesirable tenants.

So much of the religion that parades under the Christian banner has not advanced beyond the negative. There are Christians who are better known for what they are against than what they are for. They use up most of their spiritual energies saying "No!" They major on not being bad and pride themselves in what they do not do. They are known for what they denounce and what they condemn. They are true Protestants—always protesting about something!

Negative Righteousness

This attitude is known as negative righteousness. It describes those Christians who proudly broadcast, "I don't drink. I don't smoke. I don't gossip. I don't curse. I don't fornicate." To that I say, "Neither does a rock!"

Suppose you want to plant a flower garden. If all you do is weed the land, that does not produce flowers. Once you have gotten rid of the weeds, you have to plant some flowers where the weeds were or the weeds will return. Once the man got rid of the evil spirit, he should have put something positive in its place. That is why in the New Testament we are taught to deal with evil by eliminating the negative and accentuating the positive. The New Testament never closes a passage by telling us not to do something; we are also given instructions on what to do instead of something negative.

> *Do not get drunk on wine, which leads to debauchery. Instead, be filled with the Spirit.* (Ephesians 5:18, NIV)

> *This I say then, Walk in the Spirit, and ye shall not fulfil the lust of the flesh.* (Galatians 5:16, KJV)

> *Be not overcome of evil, but overcome evil with good.* (Romans 12:21, KJV)

When Jesus was asked what is the greatest commandment, He did not say, "Thou shalt not..." He accentuated the positive: "Thou shalt love the Lord thy God with all thy might, heart, soul and strength and thy neighbor as thy self."

Doctors will tell you that if you are trying to fight off some sickness, it is not enough to get rid of the cold. You then have to promote a healthy body, or the cold will come back.

In Alcoholics Anonymous, they tell you that the first step to recovery is to admit you have a problem. The second step is to submit to a higher power. Once you have eliminated the problem, however, you have to put something in its place. Therefore, the twelve step plan of AA encourages finding someone else who has an alcohol problem and showing them how they, too, can remain sober.

Being Filled with God's Power

When the man expelled the evil spirit, he needed the Holy Spirit. The evil spirits that had tormented him were idols substituting for God.

Augustine said, "Thou hast made us for Thyself, and restless is our soul until we find rest in Thee." Since we are made in God's image, we have in our hearts a God-shaped hole. This God-shaped hole will be filled with nothing and no one but God and His love.

Human beings can't stand to be empty! We need to feel full of self-worth, confidence, love. God's presence in our lives provides these needs. When we sense the presence of a void in our lives, we begin to try and fill it, "by any means necessary." When God is absent, we find ourselves depending on artificial substitutes like cocaine, alcohol, food, nicotine, sex, etc. Therefore, addiction is a form of idolatry. It attempts to put things or substances in a place where only God belongs.

When our esteem is low or we cannot face something that we feel powerless to handle, we swallow something, buy something, smoke something, or drink something to produce the illusion of what we are missing. But the illusion is a deception. It is a lie that promises release, but brings bondage. It promises fullness, but brings only emptiness. It promises to take us to heaven, but it only pushes us down to hell.

Suppose something is wrong with your car engine. There is a steady knocking sound under your hood. The transmission is going out, but you don't have the money to pay for it. Yet you need your car to get to work so you continue to drive your car. The noise not only persists, but it steadily intensifies. In order to take your mind from the knocking under the hood, you turn up the sound on your car stereo to drown out the knocking noise. The loud music does not fix the problem, it only takes your mind off it.

This is how addictions work. Something is going wrong underneath our hoods. Instead of dealing with it, we seek a diversion to drown the pain or fear out. That is why the goal of addiction recovery programs is not content simply to get people to stop drinking or drugging. The goal is to fix what is under the hood because even when people stop drinking and drugging and they tend not to deal with what's under the hood. Such a person is simply a dry drunk.

When the man did not fill the void left by the expulsion of the demon, it returned and brought along seven more demons. When we do not fill our lives with God, we have to deal with the seven demons it takes to fill that void. Those seven demons are:

Denial: Refusal to accept that you have a problem. God can't fix what you won't face.

Rationalization: Making excuses to justify your behavior.

Cover-up: Projecting a false image of competence and success while hiding the reality of who you really are.

Procrastination: Putting off dealing with the problem.

Guilt: Sadness and depression for what you have done.

Shame: Sadness and depression for what you have become.

Dehumanization: The absence of dignity. You don't care anymore, so you won't eat, wash, or comb your hair. The demon takes priority over being human.

The man cleaned up his house and got rid of the evil spirit, but his house still had a void. The house was disinfected, but depressing. The house was decorated, but desolate. Anyone facing this situation needs to know there is good news. The good news is that God wants to fill empty lives with the power of His presence.

Isaiah says that one of the things the Messiah will do is to set the captives free. The Messiah will give them beauty for ashes, oil of joy for mourning, and a garment of praise for the spirit of heaviness!

— *Musings* —

Twelve Steps to Recovery

When we practice the twelve steps of spiritual recovery, we have:

1. Admitted we were powerless over [specify addictions /compulsive behavior] and that our lives had become unmanageable.

For I know that good itself does not dwell in me, that is, in my sinful nature. For I have the desire to do what is good, but I cannot carry it out. (Romans 7:18, NIV)

2. Came to believe that a Power greater than ourselves could restore us to sanity.

For it is God who works in you to will and to act according to his good purpose. (Philippians 2:13, NIV)

3. Made a decision to turn our wills and our lives over to the care of God.

Therefore, I urge you, brothers and sisters, in view of God's mercy, to offer your bodies as a living sacrifice, holy and pleasing to God—this is your true and proper worship. (Romans 12:1, NIV)

4. Made a searching and fearless moral inventory of ourselves.

Let us examine our ways and test them, and let us return to the LORD. (Lamentations 3:40, NIV)

5. Admitted to God, to ourselves, and to another human being, the exact nature of our wrongs.

Therefore confess your sins to each other and pray for each other so that you may be healed. The prayer of a righteous person is powerful and effective. (James 5:16, NIV)

6. Were entirely ready to have God remove all these defects of character.

Humble yourselves before the Lord, and he will lift you up. (James 4:10, NIV)

7. Humbly asked Him to remove all our shortcomings.

If we confess our sins, he is faithful and just and will forgive us our sins and purify us from all unrighteousness. (1 John 1:9, NIV)

8. Made a list of all persons we had harmed, and became willing to make amends to them all.

Do to others as you would have them do to you. (Luke 6:31, NIV)

9. Made direct amends to such people whenever possible, except when to do so would injure them or others.

Therefore, if you are offering your gift at the altar and there remember that your brother has something against you, leave your gift there in front of the altar. First go and be reconciled to them; then come and offer your gift. (Matthew 5:23-24, NIV)

10. Continued to take personal inventory and when we were wrong, promptly admitted it.

So, if you think you are standing firm, be careful that you don't fall! (1 Corinthians 10:12, NIV)

11. Sought through prayer and meditation to improve our conscious contact with God, praying only for knowledge of His will for us and power to carry that out.

Let the message of Christ dwell among you richly as you teach and admonish one another with all wisdom through psalms, hymns, and songs from the Spirit, singing to God with gratitude in your hearts. (Colossians 3:16, NIV)

12. Having had a spiritual experience as the result of these steps, tried to carry this message to others and to practice these principles in all our affairs.

Brothers and sisters, if someone is caught in a sin, you who live by the Spirit should restore that person gently. But watch yourselves, or you also may be tempted. (Galatians 6:1, NIV)

— Ministries —

CAMP
The Christian Addiction Ministry Program

The purpose of CAMP is to provide spiritual support and counseling for persons who are chemically dependent. CAMP is not intended to function as a drug treatment facility. Drug treatment programs are authorized to prescribe drugs and/or extensive medical therapies. Drug counseling endeavors to help addicts realize that they have a drug problem and what they need to do about their addiction. Therefore, drug counseling is educational and directional.

The CAMP should meet twice a week, possibly Monday and Friday. The CAMP leader should be a concerned and sincere person who has a passion for helping addicts. In many instances, the CAMP leader might be a recovering addict with extensive recovery.

{*NOTE:* This program can be adapted to help persons with other addictions, including addictions to sex, food, spending, and so forth.}

Advertise CAMP

Pulpit, word-of-mouth, church bulletin announcements at the host church and area churches, newsletters, flyers, radio and television public service announcements, and community newspapers.

Conduct Saturday Night Worship Quarterly

Addicts congregate on common ground to worship God.

Lectionary Bible Study on Monday Nights

Use the *Life Recovery Bible* (Tyndale House Publishers, 1992), designed for chemically dependent people and designed for living in recovery.

Friday Night Fellowships

Host a fellowship, testimonial and sharing time—providing an opportunity for participants to share personal concern supersedes all other activities. Every chemically dependent person is the same distance away from the next drink or high.

Volunteer with a Hospital

Network with hospitals and treatment centers to find potential participants.

Share Testimonies

Allow opportunities for recovering addicts to share hope and experiences.

Invite Guest speakers

Present guest speakers monthly, including recovering addicts, psychologists, clergy, physicians, and treatment counselors.

Distribute Literature

Maintain current, updated literature, tapes, books and other resources in a recovery library or information center.

Form a Partnership with Drug Treatment Centers

Devise a plan for potential participants to enter the CAMP program upon leaving treatment facilities.

Ensure Church Involvement

Integrate CAMP participants into the church as they feel more confident and self-assured.

Identify Houses and Dealers in the Community

Identify crack houses and distribution corners. Expose terroristic, drug-related activities.

Evangelism

Create as many opportunities as possible to lead unconverted participants to salvation.

Accountability Groups

Create accountability groups so that participants can grow to depend on each other and share with each other when they face difficulties or are tempted to return to substance abuse.

— CHAPTER ELEVEN —

Values Under Construction

If you value your children,
teach them values!

He spake also this parable; A certain man had a fig tree planted in his vineyard; and he came and sought fruit thereon, and found none. Then said he unto the dresser of his vineyard, Behold, these three years I come seeking fruit on this fig tree, and find none: cut it down; why cumbereth it the ground? And he answering said unto him, Lord, let it alone this year also, till I shall dig about it, and dung it: And if it bear fruit, well: and if not, then after that thou shalt cut it down.(Luke 13:6-9, KJV)

· · · · · ·

And the contention was so sharp between them, that they departed asunder one from the other: and so Barnabas took Mark, and sailed unto Cyprus; And Paul chose Silas, and departed, being recommended by the brethren unto the grace of God. (Acts 15:39-40, KJV)

· · · · · ·

Only Luke is with me. Take Mark, and bring him with thee: for he is profitable to me for the ministry. (2 Timothy 4:11, KJV)

Have you ever given more than a passing thought to some of the messages that are contained in the road signs? The road signs we find on the streets, highways, boulevards and major thoroughfares of our cities and neighborhoods? Road signs, of course, are designed to alert motorists to what is taking place on the road, enabling them to better navigate their vehicles as they journey through traffic. Life is also a journey, from the womb to the tomb. We can take some familiar road signs and, with spiritual imagination, place them in various areas of our lives so that we might better navigate journey through the traffic of life.

Think about some of those road signs using some spiritual imagination. Some of the signs we encounter on the road are:

- Proceed with Caution

- One Way Street

- Dead End Street

- Slow—Children At Play

- Yield to the Right of Way

- Keep Right Except to Pass

- Rest Area

- Under Construction

While these road signs are designed to navigate motorists, they also speak very powerfully to our lives if we would just use spiritual imagination.

It is a fruitful exercise to take some of the familiar signs off the road and post them in key areas of our lives. For example, many marriages break up because the husband or wife won't yield the right of way. Some children are messed up because some reckless parents won't recognize the need to slow down because their children are at play. And how many lives are burned out because we won't stop and rest when our bodies give us appropriate signs? How many people don't take the time to cultivate friendships? They alienate people, whom they see as competitors, because they live life in the passing lane, and they refuse to cruise in the right lane.

There is one sign in particular, however, that we often see but perhaps don't think about much. It is a road sign that reads, "Under Construction." Whenever this road sign is displayed, it is designed to alert motorists to the fact that improvements are taking place on the road; therefore it will be necessary to exercise caution.

All of us have experienced being in traffic that is stalled while improvements are being made on the road to make the road more useable. Hopefully, all of us can say about our lives that we are under construction. Probably we all have experienced some potholes in our personality, but we're under construction. The very knowledge that we are under construction can help us not become too despondent when we fail to achieve the level of maturity and growth that we desire.

Being under construction also should release us from a spirit of being judgmental. When our friends and family members disappoint us because they are under construction. It helps us to get up after we've fallen down because we know that God is not through with us yet either. Being under construction allows us to celebrate with the apostle John who wrote:

> *Beloved, now are we the sons of God, and it doth not yet ap-pear what we shall be: but we know that, when he shall ap-pear, we shall be like him; for we shall see him as he is.* (1 John 3:2, KJV)

Being under construction means that today's setback does not necessarily block tomorrow's achievement. It means that counting someone out or giving up on someone is always premature because we are under construction. The concept of being under construction is very well illustrated in 2 Timothy.

The apostle Paul was in real need. He was on death row in a drafty prison, wrapped in tattered and ragged clothing. He was aging, his health was failing, and his eyesight dim. To make matters worse, he had been abandoned in his most critical hour by his closest friends and colleagues. In desperation he wrote to his trusted and faithful lieutenant, Timothy. He wrote to him with an urgent plea for help. He told Timothy, "Do your best to come to me quickly, and when you come, bring with you the coat that I left in Troas with Carpus. Also bring my books and my parchments. And on your way, go by and pick up Mark and bring him with you, because Mark is very helpful to me for my ministry."

The words "go get Mark and bring him for he is profitable to my ministry" illustrate how God is able to reconstruct and build up our lives to useful service. Twelve years previously, the last thing Paul would have said was "get Mark and bring him with you for he is profitable to my ministry." Twelve years earlier, Mark was a dismal failure. Now he had become profitable. Twelve years earlier Paul and that great missionary, Barnabas, were commissioned by the church at Antioch to take an expedition into the non-Jewish world and open new frontiers for the gospel. On that first missionary journey, they were accompanied by a young man named Mark, who happened to be the nephew of Barnabas.

While they were on the first phase of their preaching tour, they prepared to climb the rough and steep Taurus Mountains—known to be infested with bandits. Mark, upon seeing the mountains, turned back and went home.

Mark packed up his Snoop Dog CD's, his Ultra Sheen, and his brush and comb into his duffel bag and went back home to his mother. Now, why Mark went back home we really do not know. Some scholars have speculated that Mark went back home because he was homesick. He was too tied to his mother's apron strings—she being a very prominent woman named Mary. He had never done anything as rigorous as he was doing with Paul and Barnabas. Others have suggested that he went back home because he was upset, angry with a partnership that had developed between Barnabas and Paul. When they had started out, it was a partnership of Barnabus and Paul. But soon Paul began to eclipse Barnabas, and it became a partnership of Paul and Barnabas. Perhaps Mark did not like this arrangement and decided to go home. Or maybe he wasn't down for evangelizing non-Jews, and he could not stomach the idea of bringing persons into the faith who were not of Jewish stock. Perhaps, it was due to an ideological or philosophical difference, and he decided to go back home. We will never know the real reason why Mark left. All we ever know is that on the first phase of the journey, Paul and Barnabas were facing the mountains.

Paul and Barnabas went on in spite of Mark, and they had great success on their first missionary journey. They preached Christ in strange places, and they planted churches in strategic locations. Because of what they did, a door was opened for the advancement of the gospel throughout the ancient world. Everyone at the Antioch church was excited about what Paul and Barnabas had done. In fact, even the conservative Jerusalem church was excited. They had a conference and voted to affirm the work of Paul and Barnabas. Everyone in church was so happy about the accomplishments of Paul and Barnabas that they had a great celebration.

After the Jerusalem Conference and the celebration, Paul and Barnabas decided to revisit the churches they had established on their first missionary journey. The purpose of their second missionary journey was to strengthen and encourage these young churches. But in the midst of Paul, Barnabas and the church making preparations for their journey, the excitement of their hub of activity was broken when Mark showed up. With a duffel bag in his hand, Mark told Paul and Barnabas, "Yes, I messed up the first time, but let bygones be bygones."

We all make mistakes. Mark wanted to present himself on their second missionary journey. Paul didn't like that idea. Paul felt that the mission was too important, that what they were trying to accomplish was too urgent, and that Mark had proven to be too immature. So Paul said, "No, Mark, you cannot go with us because if you did, you would be in the way." Paul sternly rejected the idea of Mark's accompanying them.

Barnabas, on the other hand, was a bit more soft. He had more compassion for young Mark. He told Paul, "Yes, Mark messed up. Yes, Mark turned back, but we've all messed up. We've all made mistakes. Let's give him another chance. In fact Paul, you've messed up in your life. Come on man, cut him a little slack!"

Paul was unyielding. He said, "No! Mark will only be in the way. He needs to grow up. He's too immature. His mother has smothered him and he just can't go."

It's ironic that Paul, who received grace himself, who preached grace, and who championed grace, was not willing to extend grace to Mark for his previous mistake. Is Paul's message of grace just a vocal message, or is it a vital message? Is it mere rhetoric or is it real? Was Paul so concerned with his work in missions that he was unconcerned with the missionary worker named Mark?

It has been said that the Church and Christians alike can contract four diseases:

1. *Sleeping sickness*—Occurs when all types of needs exist in the community, but the church is asleep to the needs that are present.

2. *Cirrhosis of the giver*—Christians who walk out during the offering, or hide under their pews, or they put a dollar in and ask the usher for seventy-five cents change back!

3. *Spiritual myopia*—Christians who are myopic can't see. They don't have a vision of what they can become.

4. *Hardening of the arteries*—This is what has happened to Christians who don't speak to certain folk, are not kind to folks, have their noses up in the air, or are who are mean to folks. They don't love folks and extend to them the same grace that God has given to all believers.

Cheap Grace Versus Costly Grace

Could it be that, while Paul didn't have sleeping sickness, and while he didn't have cirrhosis of the giver, and while he didn't have spiritual myopia, Paul was experiencing hardening of the arteries? We don't know. But what we do know is that whatever Paul's motive was, his decision that Mark could not go, split up the greatest missionary team that Christian history has ever known. The result of their difference of opinion about Mark was that Paul and Barnabas went their separate ways. Paul took Silas with him and went to Syria and Cilicia. Barnabas took Mark and preached in Cypress.

This is the last we read of Mark until twelve years later when Paul was facing death at the hands of the wicked emperor Nero. From his prison cell, Paul wrote to Timothy, asking for his coat, his books and his parchments, and, wonder of wonders, Mark "because he is profitable to me in the ministry."

Mark, who had one time been judged worthless, had by now proven himself worthy. He must have been under construction. Mark, who twelve years earlier was useless, found usefulness in his work. Mark, who at one time was seen as a liability, was now an asset to the ministry. Mark, a young man who was once in the way, was now on his way to assist a man who always felt that he was in the way. He must have been under construction.

But what has happened? How did Paul come to change his opinion of Mark? How did Paul come to believe in the usefulness of this man whom he once felt was worthless? Did Paul's current condition cause him to change? Was he so desperate that he would settle for anyone, including Mark? Did he call on Mark because, after twelve years, Paul had mellowed out and lowered his standards? I don't think so. I believe the reason Paul changed his opinion of Mark was because during those twelve years, Mark changed. Mark grew and matured. Mark was under construction.

Paul didn't lower his standards. In his critical situation, he didn't need a spineless, limp-toed wimp around him. When we are in trouble, we don't need trouble to come along with us. When we're facing our own troubles, we can be miserable all by ourselves. Additionally, there were others Paul could have called upon to assist him. He could have called Onesimus. He was associated with Tychicus. He could have called Silas. He could have called Epaphroditus of Philippi. But he didn't call Silas and he didn't call Onesimus and he didn't call Epaphroditus. Instead, Paul said, "When you come, Timothy, bring Mark because Mark is profitable for me in my ministry."

Paul was now calling for the same Mark who had once deserted him and Barnabas. Paul wanted the young man who once had played the coward's role. Paul asked for the Mark who left Paul and Barnabas when they were facing those rough mountains. But Paul needed Mark as he was facing Nero. The reason Paul wanted Mark was not because Paul lowered his standards; it was because Mark raised his performance.

Paul preached grace; but he didn't preach cheap grace. Paul preached costly grace. Cheap grace would have lowered the standard in order to accommodate Mark. Costly grace says, "Mark, you grow up to meet the standards, and then we'll give you another chance." When a teacher practices cheap grace, she says to a Mark, "I'm going to grade the test on a curve." But costly grace is when a teacher says, "Mark, turn off the TV at night, get rid of the Nintendo and study, because I know you can do better and I want you to reach your best." Cheap grace is when people are allowed to do just anything because not much is expected of them. But costly grace is when people are required to go under construction, maturing, developing and becoming all that God wants them to become.

Somewhere between Acts 15 and 2 Timothy 4—somewhere between the time when Paul was facing the mountains and when Paul was facing Nero, Mark was under construction. Mark matured. He grew up and became a man. And as cruel as it might sound, sometimes we need a stern, strict, demanding voice in our lives. We need a voice like Paul's saying, "Mark, I'm not going to baby you. I'm not going to carry you. I'm not going to make excuses for you. Mark, grow up and become a man. Then come back."

I believe every African American needs to go see the movie entitled, *Higher Learning*. If you haven't seen it, rent the video. In the movie is a black political science professor who has high standards. There is also a black athlete in the movie who believed that just because he was the only black student in this black professor's class, the professor was going to cut him some slack. But the athlete hadn't paid his dues. So the professor called him to the front of the class and said, "You can't take my class because you haven't paid your dues."

The athlete started saying, "Well, you don't understand how tough it is. I'm a black man from the 'hood who grew up in poverty and on welfare. You ought to have some pity on me."

The professor said, "No pity. If you don't reach the standard, then get out of school!"

Because the professor had standards that were unyielding, the boy was forced to use his own creativity. Somehow, he found some money to pay for the tuition. He entered the class; he grasped some of the ideas, but his grammar was not right. The professor gave him poor grades. Again he went to the professor and said, "Come on, brother man, you're one of the brothers."

The professor replied, "You ain't my brother, man. Ain't no brother 'thang' in my class. You've got to have it right. You not only have to conceptualize it right, but you have to write it down just right!"

The boy left the class, calling the teacher "Uncle Tom, Clarence Thomas, you make me sick! You must be listening to Rush Limbaugh!"

He left the class unyielding, but the professor was equally unyielding. But the student met a nice, studious girlfriend, and together they worked hard, burned the midnight oil, went to the library and studied. The next time the student submitted a paper, it was correct because the professor didn't lower his standards to accommodate mediocrity. Instead, the boy raised his standards to meet the demands of the professor.

Unfortunately, many of us parents are crippling our children because we make too many excuses and too many allowances for mediocre behavior. There is no excuse! We need to tell our kids, "Turn off the video games, get rid of your Power Rangers, and burn the midnight oil."

Our children must grow up knowing that no matter how racist a teacher is, if that teacher asks, "What is two plus two, the answer will be four." It doesn't matter if the teacher is wearing a Ku Klux Klan uniform; that teacher cannot stop a student who makes the grade.

African Americans need to grow up. We need to mature. As we strive toward maturity, we must keep in mind that maturity is more than just growing old. There are plenty of old immature folks. Gray hair does not equate to maturity. There's a whole lot of gray hair covering the heads of immature people. There are a whole lot of people who grow old, but never grow up. Maturation is the art of fulfilling one's purpose. Maturity is when we become what God intended and designed us to become. When we're focused on that goal, then we're maturing.

In nature, God has a purpose for everything. Consider the sun, a big luminous ball in our sky. It radiates heat, light and energy. Every morning the sun lights up and heats the earth. The sun looks to God and says, "This is the purpose for which you made me. I'm just maturing, doing what you told me to do and being all that you wanted me to be."

God's answer to the sun is, "Well done, sun!"

There is seed on the earth. The seed on the earth looks to the sun and says, "Thank you, sun, because God made me to be a tree, but I can't be all that I'm supposed to be if you're not what you're supposed to be."

The seed looks at God and says, "God, you made me to be a tree, and I won't be satisfied as a seed until I become all you want me to be." And the seed grows up and becomes a tree.

God looks at the tree and replies, "Well done, seed. You are maturing because you have fulfilled your purpose."

After the tree develops, the tree looks at God and says, "Well God, what do you want me to do?"

And God says, "Well, tree, I made you to produce apples, and you're not maturing if you don't produce apples." It doesn't matter how many designer labels are on your leaves. I don't care if you've got Florsheims on your roots. If God designed you to be an apple tree, but you're not producing apples, then you're not becoming all God intended you to become. So the tree produces apples.

So when apples appear on the tree, they say, "God for what purpose did you make us? You had a purpose for the sun, a purpose for the seed, and a purpose for the tree, but we are apples."

God tells them, "If you look at the chemical composition of yourselves, I put vitamins in you so that you could nourish human beings. Remember, you're not going to be all that you can be unless someone puts you in his system."

And the apple says, "Thank you, God," and gets off the tree.

Then the man who ate the apples looks at God and says, "You had a purpose for the sun, a purpose for the seed, a purpose for the tree; you had a purpose for the apples, but what about me?"

And God answers the many by saying, "This is your purpose. I made you in My image. When I formed you I made you. I put my nostrils against your nostrils and blew into them the breath of life.

You're supposed to be great! Nobody can stop you! If there is a door in your way, you can go through it. If it's closed, go under it, go over it, go around it, or find a window. No one on earth can get in your way. Be all that you can be!"

But you know what the man says to God? "I don't think so, God."

All of the other creations of nature respond affirmatively to God's purpose. But human beings go home like Mark and just sit down. Or we get in our cars and go to HBO's *Def Comedy Jam*, still not fulfilling our purpose.

God has more in mind for us than making fun of ourselves on HBO. God has something for each one of us to do. God has a gift that He wants every individual to cultivate. God has given all the saints a gift. God has something for us to do, and we're not maturing unless we are fulfilling our purpose, doing all that God wants us to do.

God has a song for you to sing. Are you singing your song? God has a sermon for you to preach. Are you preparing to preach it? God has a disease for somebody to heal. Are you in medical school learning how to cure it? God has something for black women to do besides sitting home watching soap operas. God has something for black men to do besides standing around decorating street corners. God has something for African Americans to do instead of making excuses, smoking dope, snorting coke, playing musical beds with multiple sex partners, and hanging around with negative people. God has so much more to offer!

God has more in store than we can envision! So zip up your pants, young men! Young ladies, put on your panties. God has more for you to do. Car-jacking, crack selling, pants hanging, beeper having, Ebonics speaking black folks need to know that God has more in store for our people! These images do not reflect our heritage and culture, and they nourish a slave consciousness that hinders progress. Be like Mark. Be under construction! Mark, who once had been a quitter and failure, was now a great help to the apostle Paul. But in spite of Mark's help, Paul was still executed. Mark went from helping Paul to helping Peter, according to 1 Timothy.

Tradition says that Peter also was executed. And as the Church moved to the close of the first century, someone recognized that they were facing a serious dilemma. All of the first witnesses to the historical Jesus were passing off the scene, meaning there were no more eyewitnesses to what Jesus had done. Peter, who had been on the Mount of Transfiguration with Jesus, had died. All the other disciples who had seen Jesus speak to the winds and the waves, were passing off the scene. Those disciples who saw Jesus resurrected from the grave had gone on to glory.

Since all the apostles and disciples were becoming extinct, the question was, "What are we going to do to preserve the record and memory for posterity of what Jesus did?" Mark, who had once been a quitter and possibly a whiner, stepped up to the plate and said, "I've got an idea."

Because of Mark's journey and his idea, we can know the true definition of maturity; we can read the twenty-seven books of the New Testament. They are all good, like those written by the apostle John, including Revelation that talks about future events. And other good books like 1 and 2 Thessalonians and Ephesians that talk about unity—one faith, one Lord and one baptism. But one book, the first gospel, the Book of Mark, was written by this same man who had once been a quitter and once been a deserter. The reason Mark grew from being a quitter to a gospel writer was because he was under construction.

What about you? Do you want the Lord to work on you? Don't focus on the people you think need to be changed—not your mother, not your father, not your sister, not your brother, not the preacher, not the deacon, not the choir members, but you!

If you want to be under construction, work on your hands so you can do His lifting. Work on your mind so you can think right. Work on your feet so you can walk right. Work on your heart so you can feel right. Work on your mind and your body. Work on your finances or your relationship with your children, or work on your marriage. Whatever you do, work! Tell those around you to proceed with caution because you are under construction!

— *Musings* —

Answer these questions:

- As you reflect over the last twelve years of your life, what are some positive changes in your life that indicate you have been under construction?

- Paul exercised tough love in the life of John Mark. How can we exercise tough love to people we care about without being uncaring and unsympathetic? Is there a difference between tough love and being tough?

- The times when someone exercised tough love on you, what correlation do you see between their tough love and your personal maturity?

- Barnabas exercised grace toward John Mark. When does costly grace become cheap grace?

- During the twelve silent years of John Mark's metamorphosis, what do you think John Mark was doing to have emerged so mature?

- What effect might Paul's rejection of John Mark have had on his self-esteem and confidence?

- How do you think John Mark responded when Timothy went by and gave Paul's message?

- Maturity has been defined as the act of fulfilling one's God-ordained purpose. What is your God-ordained purpose in life? How are you fulfilling it?

- Paul asked John Mark for help. Perhaps one of the greatest needs is the need to be needed. How does being needed build one's sense of self-worth?

— *Ministries* —

Character Education and Development Initiative (CEDI)

One of the fundamental problems afflicting urban youth is the pervasiveness of moral illiteracy that results in their inability to effectively cope with life challenges and to distinguish right from wrong. The Character Education and Development Initiative is designed to reinforce moral literacy. This initiative needs adult volunteers who have an interest in youth and a desire to see them mature morally.

The moral development of youth and children is extremely important. We determine what kind of society we will have by the morals we teach our children. Therefore, in an age of moral relativism, CEDI will seek to give youth a moral compass that will navigate them through the maze of moral decay and decadence that pervades our society.

Basically, there are four levels on which people can live:

The Instinctive Level: This is the level of urges and passions. To live on this level is to give free expression to our natural urges.

The Cultural Level: This is when we do what is expected by the culture in which we live. For youth, this would mean peer pressure. The motivation of life on this level is to be approved, affirmed and accepted by the peer group. Therefore, the group decides what is right and what is wrong, and we simply conform to group consensus.

The Conscience Level: This is when a person determines what is right and wrong because of his or her independent convictions.

The Christian Level: This is the highest level. On this level, the final test for every decision concerning right or wrong is Christ. Many young people wear WWJD (What Would Jesus Do?) paraphernalia. God's Word will be the final authority for determining right from wrong.

The Character Education and Development Initiative is designed to help young people develop morally by empowering them to make Christ their moral reference point.

CEDI Requirements

- Adults who are concerned about morals and who want to help youth acquire moral standards from a Christian perspective.

- The Bible, *The Book of Virtues* and *The Moral Compass* by William J. Bennett; *Would You Rather...?* by Doug Fields; and *The African American Book of Values*, by Steven Barboza.

- Parental Involvement. Each month participants in the CEDI will explore the significance of a different virtue.

JANUARY: Altruism

Definition

Working for the good of others and not simply self.

Biblical Example

The Good Samaritan (Luke 10:29-37). Rejoice always in the Lord (Philippians 2:4)

Objective

Participants will understand the importance of treating others right.

Action Plan

1. Engage participants in activities that help other young people without providing any direct benefit in return.

2. Provide materials for participants to make gifts for nursing home residents.

3. Organize participants so they can conduct a "designer" clothing drive and give clothing to children and young people they do not know.

4. Study the lives of altruistic people.

FEBRUARY: Justice

Definition

Fairness

Biblical Example

Moses (Exodus—Deuteronomy); Zaccheus (Luke 19:1-11)

Objective

To help youth recognize and appreciate fairness as a virtue and to practice it in their daily living.

Action Plan

1. Conduct a mock trial.

2. Interview a judge.

3. Identify historical examples of justice.

MARCH: Responsibility

Definition

Being accountable for one's attitudes, actions, chores and behaviors.

Biblical Example

David (1 Samuel 16—1 Kings 1); the Paralytic at Bethesda (John 5:2 15)

Objective

To help youth assume responsibility for their actions and personal behaviors.

Action Plan

1. Analyze the relationship between rights and responsibilities.

2. Participate in a community service project.

3. Lead a discussion on the dangers of blaming and excuse making.

4. Lead a discussion on responsibility from the recommended text.

APRIL: Knowledge

Definition

Lifelong learning that contributes to quality of life and career success.

Biblical Example

Jesus grew in wisdom, stature, and favor, with God and man (Luke 2:52)

Objective

Participants will realize that success in life is dependent upon acquiring knowledge.

Action Plan

1. Listen to adults in various professions/occupations describe the knowledge and skills they employ on their jobs.

2. Play a game in the same manner as "Jeopardy" using the knowledge they learn in class.

3. Conduct a panel discussion on current events in the community, in the nation, and around the world.

4. Read about knowledge in the recommended books.

MAY: Honesty

Definition

A life characterized by integrity, trust, and truthfulness.

Biblical Example

Live so others will see your work and glorify God (1 Peter 2:12)

Objective

Participants will see the benefits of honesty and will recognize the consequences of their actions—whether positive or negative.

Action Plan

1. Create a script and costumes, and perform a contemporary version of Pinnochio.

2. Engage participants in role play, acting out honesty and/or truthfulness.

3. Lead in a discussion on why honesty is the best policy.

4. Read passages about honesty in the recommended books.

JUNE: Courtesy

Definition

Polite and helpful actions demonstrated through sharing, amicability, cordiality, thoughtfulness and respect.

Biblical Example

David and Mephibosheth (2 Samuel 9:1-7)

Objective

Participants will begin to demonstrate courteous behavior at home, at church, at school and in the community.

Action Plan

1. Have participants make a list of twenty-five of the most discourteous things youth are presently doing.

2. Devise a list of twenty-five ways to demonstrate courtesy.

3. Participants will commit to practicing two courteous behaviors each week and report their progress to the class.

4. Read about courtesy in books from the recommended reading list.

JULY: Human Worth

Definition

The importance of seeing everyone as important and treating people as you would like to be treated.

Biblical Example

Jesus and Bartimaeus (Mark 10:46-52)

Objective

Participants will begin to value all of humanity and to treat all persons with dignity and worth.

Action Plan

1. Students should write positive comments about each other.

2. Invite physically challenged persons to the class to talk about their lives and how many people view the physically challenged.

3. Read and lead a discussion on human worth from the recommended text books.

AUGUST: Courage

Definition

The commitment to do the right thing when facing times of stress, danger and adversity.

Biblical Example

Shadrach, Meshach, and Abednego (Daniel 3); Daniel in the Lions' Den (Daniel 6)

Objective

To cultivate youth who have convictions so that they will not abandon them in times of adversity.

Action Plan

1. Interview persons who have exhibited courage in the community.

2. Develop a "profiles in courage" committee that annually bestows an award of bravery to one or more deserving youth

(it may be necessary to establish two categories—younger youth: 12-15; and older youth: 16-18).

3. Guide participants to share instances when they had to exercise courage.

4. Lead participants in a discussion on courage from the recommended text books.

SEPTEMBER: Forgiveness

Definition

The ability to cancel and pardon another for wrongs they have committed against you.

Biblical Example

Jesus on the cross (Matthew 27:27-50; Mark 15:16-37; Luke 23:20-46; John 19:15-35); the stoning of Stephen (Acts 7:55-8:2)

Objective

Participants will understand the importance of moving beyond their hurts and reconciling whenever possible.

Action Plan

1. Conduct an open discussion with youth about how people have hurt them and how Christians are to respond to when hurt by others. Do we forgive and forget? Is there a difference between forgiveness and reconciliation?

2. Work with participants to develop an action plan to help youth deal with their own guilt and to forgive themselves.

3. Choose a day when youth will pledge to turn in their guns and any other weapons they might have. Advertise this day in the community and ask students to encourage others to turn in their weapons.

4. Lead participants in a discussion on forgiveness, based upon the life of Martin Luther King, Jr.

OCTOBER: Citizenship

Definition

A commitment to democratic ideals and the well-being of one's community.

Biblical Example

Christian submission to authority (Romans 13:1-7)

Objectives

Student will recognize that they not only have rights, but responsibilities to home, church, school and community.

Action Plan

1. Help youth to discuss and develop personal roles and responsibilities for home, church, school and society.
2. Invite an elected official to engage participants and talk about community responsibility.
3. Sponsor a voter registration campaign.
4. Lead participants in a discussion on citizenship from the recommended text books.

NOVEMBER: Respect

Definition

Showing honor and consideration for self, others, and one's natural environment.

Biblical Example

The greatest commandment (Matthew 22:35-40)

Objectives

Participants will discover how to develop and maintain a respectable image in their speech, dress, conduct, and actions.

Action Plan

1. Lead participants in a discussion on appropriate dress in specific and various settings and environments.

2. Develop and post a list of in-church behaviors that the youth agree are appropriate or inappropriate. Talk about about why each action is appropriate or inappropriate.

3. Teach participants respect for their church environment by planning an "operation clean-up" in and around your church.

4. Guide participants in a discussion on respect from the recommended text book.

December: Self-Discipline

Definition

The ability to properly manage and control one's temper, appetites, passions, and impulses.

Biblical Example

Parable of the Talents (Matthew 25:15-30)

Objectives

Participants will recognize the importance of taking responsibility for controlling themselves, which includes completing tasks, obeying rules, and doing their work without being reminded.

Action Plan

1. Ask participants to write down their goals and what they have to do to reach those goals.

2. Invite a successful young adult to discuss the importance and benefits of self-discipline in the lives of young people. The motivator might be an athlete or entertainer.

3. Lead participants in a discussion on diet and fitness, financial planning, and delayed gratification in order to pursue a goal.

4. Lead participants in a discussion on self-discipline, based upon recommended text books.

— CHAPTER TWELVE —

One Is a Whole Number

Two are better than one; because they have a good reward for their labour. For if they fall, the one will lift up his fellow: but woe to him that is alone when he falleth; for he hath not another to help him up. Again, if two lie together, then they have heat: but how can one be warm alone? (Ecclesiastes 4:9-11, KJV)

No task requires more strength, courage and endurance than the awesome responsibility of being a single parent. Single parents have the great challenge of performing a task alone that God intended for two. It was God's original intent that children be reared in a loving home, having continuous interaction with both a mother and a father.

In Genesis 1:28, God instructed the male and the female to "be fruitful and multiply." As you read the passage, you will notice that God gave the first couple a two-fold assignment. The latter command, to "multiply," refers to biological reproduction. The former command, to be "fruitful," refers to the parent's responsibility to nurture their children—physically, intellectually, spiritually and socially, as well as their total environment.

We tend to read the words "fruitful" and "multiply" as though they are a repetition of the same thing (Hebrew parallelism). However, they refer to two different activities. It is possible to multiply and not be fruitful in your multiplication. God was saying to both the male and the female, "Don't just make babies (multiply). Be sure to develop (fruitful) what you have conceived."

The same message is reinforced in Deuteronomy 6:4-8, in what is known as the Shema. The word *Shema* means "to hear." It is the Hebrew statement of faith that declares that Israel's God is One. God has given Jewish parents the responsibility of passing this theological tenet on to their children. This centers the religious instruction of children in the home by their parents.

In Jeremiah 29-5-7, Jeremiah instructed the men living in Babylonian exile to take wives and develop strong families. From the perspective of Jeremiah, the way to survive and prosper during the horrors of Babylonian captivity was through developing stable, two-parent families.

The supreme example of God's intent for two-parent families is the life of Jesus. For at least the first twelve years of Jesus' life, He was reared in a two-parent home. Having both a mother and a father to nurture Him created healthy, balanced growth in His life. Luke 2:52 says that Jesus grew in wisdom, (intellectually), stature (physically), favor with God (spiritually), and favor with man (socially).

Throughout American history, the effects of racism often have prevented African Americans from maintaining the stable family dynamic that the Bible mandates. During Slavery, black families had no legal status and could be dissolved at any time at the discretion of the slave master. This required the slave community to develop coping mechanisms in order to survive. In cases where parents were sold or separated from their children, the other men and women in the slave community stepped in to share in parenting responsibilities for the orphaned children. The practice of taking in children changed the definition of the word parent in the slave community to mean "all adults."

At the beginning of the twentieth century, the black family had demonstrated such remarkable resiliency to stay together that 90 percent of all black families had a male father figure present. However, by the 1960s, a trend developed that saw the removal of the black male parent in the home. In 1965, U.S. Assistant Secretary of Labor Daniel Patrick Moynihan argued that the main crisis facing the black community was the deterioration of the black family unit due to the rise of female-headed households. Children raised in single parent households were more inclined to live in poverty and had other social dysfunctionalities to a greater extent than children raised in two-parent homes.

At the time of the Moynihan report, 50 percent of all black children were born to unwed mothers. At the dawn of the 21st Century, that number had escalated to 70 percent. Critics of Moynihan argued that he placed the blame for the decline of the black family on internal pathologies in the black family and not on the external realities of racism.

Sociologist Nathan Hare has observed that less time should be spent on trying to determine the causes of the ills to the black family and more energy and time must be used to find solutions to the problem. One solution is to first come to grips with the fact that we have a serious problem in the black community. This problem is at the root of most of the problems facing the black community. As the family goes, so goes the community. Leadership in the black community must acknowledge that while racism does exist, racism does not leave a people without moral autonomy. Single parent households cannot be accepted as the norm in the black community. We must rediscover the same spirit that our ancestors possessed during slavery to keep and maintain strong, two-parent families.

The biblical ideal of two-parent (mother and father) families is currently being challenged by those who are advocating an alternative to the traditional family. America is presently engaged in a culture war to determine the moral direction of the nation. The main battle front on which this war is being waged is concerning the issue of family. In the early 1990s, on the television program *Murphy Brown*, the high profile television reporter proudly had a baby out of wedlock. She proclaimed that fathers were no longer needed except as sperm donors. Since then, more women have followed suit; for example, Madonna has, on two occasions, made a choice to become a single mother.

It is important that the Church not be silent about this issue. The Church must teach and preach God's will for the family. The single parent family is not God's design nor God's intent. That is not to say, however, that single parent families are not real families. This assertion is instead simply a recognition of divine intent and the need for the Church to develop strategies to empower and assist single parents in the arduous task of child rearing. The Church must never put itself in the position of placing additional burdens on single parents by putting them on guilt trips.

There are a number of reasons why people become single parents:

1. **Single parents by date:** The date I am referring to is a sex date. In cases where pregnancy results from a casual sexual liaison, usually the pregnancy was not deliberate or planned. In some instances, however, pregnancy is the planned and deliberate goal of one of the parties involved. Statistics tell us that "single by date" is the number one way that people in the black community become single parents.

2. **Single parent by divorce:** Divorce is on the rise in America. Almost 50 percent of all marriages end in divorce. "Until death do us part" has become "until dissatisfaction do we part." The Church must do everything possible to strengthen marriages, especially through the difficult times that are an inevitable part of matrimony.

3. **Single parent by desertion:** Many men (and sometimes women) simply abdicate their parental responsibility. It is important that we hold parents accountable for the care, nurture, and protection of their children. Caring for our children is not the responsibility of the government. Parenting is the responsibility of those two persons who were responsible for the conception of the child. The Bible says that anyone who will not take care of his or her own family is worse than an infidel. Even when couples divorce, there is no excuse for divorcing oneself from one's obligation to one's children.

4. **Single parent by decision:** Many black singles have decided to make room in their hearts and budgets for children in need of a home via adoption or foster parenting. These magnanimous men and women have made a decision to become parents but not spouses. This noble decision must be applauded and encouraged through tangible means of support. Adoptive families represent the best of the black tradition of extended families that dates back to Africa. A disproportionate number of black children are waiting for

adoption. In some instances, whites are leading blacks in the adoption of black children. Single parenting by decision is noble. There is still a need for adoptive/foster parents to have a familial support system and not try to do it alone. That support system may include family members, friends, church ministries and other agencies or support groups. Parenting is a job that was intended for two. The person who singly tries to handle a job designed for two people is courting stress and frustration.

5. **Single parent by death:** Although child-rearing was designed for two, the reality of death sometimes reduces the responsibility of parenting to one. My mother died when I was the age of eleven. I had three other sisters, ranging from ages 5-16. My father became a single parent through death. I often think about what would have happened to me and my sisters if my mother had been a single parent. My father secured the presence of my aunt who stayed with us until my father remarried, providing us with a wonderful new mother and caregiver who brought to our lives the nurture and stability that we needed.

Life is fragile for all of us. David said, "There is just one step between me and death." We cannot determine when death will come; nevertheless, it is important that we practice healthy life-styles to reduce the risk of death through diseases that can be avoided in the first place. Maintaining good health is a part of good parenting. It is important that parents take care of themselves for their children's' sake. This is especially true for African American males, who die at an earlier age than any other racial or gender group in America.

The uncompromising theme of this chapter is that parenting was intended by God for two. That is not to allege, however, that a household headed by a single parent is less than a home. Unless they are able to get some help from family members, friends, and a strong singles' ministry, single parents will experience many stresses that functioning two parent homes will not.

Parenting is always a difficult proposition, even for healthy two-parent homes. It is difficult to raise children without simultaneously raising your blood pressure! Someone once asked, "When does life begin?" Does life begin at thirty? forty? or fifty? Someone else responded by saying, "Life begins when the dog dies and all the children move out!"

Ask a group of single parents what it feels like to be a single parent, and you will be bombarded with responses like *overwhelmed, guilty, exhausted, insecure, lonely*, and *financially overextended*

Since parenting is a two-person assignment, the church must find ways to assist single parents. The writer of Ecclesiastes says, "Two are better than one...woe be unto the person who is alone" (Ecclesiastes 4:9-10).

Parenting: A Job for Two

Beyond the fact that God designed the family to include a mother and a father, there are some practical reasons why children need two parents. First, children have varied needs that a single parent will find difficult to meet alone. Every parent has strengths and weaknesses. In two parent homes, husbands and wives are able to supplement each other's weaknesses and reinforce each other's strengths.

For example, in my family, my parental role is that of a motivator and entertainer. My wife is more of a nurturer who has a gift for taking care of details. Whenever I am out-of-town, my wife tells me to hurry home because of the fun and excitement I bring to our children. However, when my wife is out-of-town, she is equally missed because the structure and discipline in our home seems to collapse. Therefore, we complement each other in areas where the other parent is not equally gifted.

Since single parents must attempt to be all things to their children, it is imperative that they be aware of their strengths and weaknesses in order to seek help from family members, church ministries and members, neighbors and friends in order to support them in areas where they are not equally gifted.

A second reason why parenting is a two-person job is because children are demanding beings. Single parents have to work outside the home, taxi children, and then cook, clean, wash, check homework, and repair broken items around the house. Nothing is more difficult for a single parent than going to work and leaving a sick child home or in someone else's care.

When all of these demands cascade upon a single parent at once, it is easy for the single parent to become "psycho mom" or "psycho dad." In addition to these time consuming demands, single parents need social outlets and personal time for themselves.

A third reason why parenting is a job designed for two is that having two parents in the home provides checks and balances for each other's decisions. Many times when my children request things, I say to them, "Go ask your mother." Their classic response is, "She told us to ask you."

Two are better than one when deciding what is best for a child. It is possible for one parent to be blind in a certain area of decision-making and in need of the wisdom that the other parent will bring. For single parents, decision-making can be supplemented through extended family members, friends and participating in singles' ministries in the church.

A fourth reason why parenting is a job designed for two is because women were not intended to be fathers and men were not intended to be mothers. In spite of our society's move toward unisexualization, women and men see life from different perspectives. There are certain contributions to a child's development and socialization that are better nurtured by a mother and the same is true of a father. For the single parent, the role of the absent parent can be supplemented through family members, friends and singles' ministries in the church.

Bring Out the Best in Your Child

During Slavery, Frederick Douglass observed that the difference between black children and white children was that white children were born into the world while black children were damned into the world. The same can be said for many children today. Some children are born into the world while others are damned into the world. To be damned into the world has nothing to do with being born black, poor or physically challenged, but instead it has to do with what parents and teachers expect from the children for whom they are responsible.

Black children from a single parent household are damned when teachers and caregivers expect less of them.

Expectation is an essential factor in determining what children achieve. What we expect becomes a self-fulfilling prophecy. If we don't expect much, we won't get much. If we don't expect children to learn, achieve and live productive lives, they won't. If all we expect from black children is poor academic performance and bad behavior, that is exactly what we get unless someone or something intervenes.

This is where current leadership in the black community is failing black youth. We have lowered the expectations of black children. When black children perform poorly in school and in society, we let them off the hook and blame racism or poverty as though these evil twins leave one morally without choices.

In 1 Chronicles 4:9-10, there is an interesting story about a man named Jabez who was the product of a single parent home. The name *Jabez* means "sorrowful." It was not a nickname; rather it was his real name—the one that appeared on his birth certificate. Imagine having to answer to the name Sorrowful. Imagine having to be introduced as Sorrowful. Day and night, you are called Sorrowful. "Go out and cut the grass, Sorrowful." Or, "Come and eat dinner, Sorrowful." What makes Jabez's name so tragic is that it was not given to him by an enemy or a stranger, but by his own mother. The Hebrew verb suggests continuous action. That means his mother continued to call her son "Sorrowful."

It has been said that the hand that rocks the cradle rules the world. It can also be added, however, that the hand that rocks the cradle can also ruin the world. The story of Jabez is a classic example of a child who had been damned into the world because all his mother expected from him was sorrow.

In the culture of the Bible, names meant something. They were more than an appellation flippantly assigned to a son or daughter simply because it sounded good. Names held meaning. They reflected something about the character of the person who possessed it. Therefore, the fact that Jabez was named Sorrowful by his own mother suggested that she did not expect much of him.

She, no doubt, expected him to use ebonics and hang out with gangs on the corner. She expected him to become a teenage father and a statistic in the Jerusalem judicial system. Many parents are still naming their children Jabez. Many schools look at black children and call them, Jabez.

Why did this mother name her own son Jabez? The text says that she bore him in sorrow. It is easy to reconstruct what happened. Since his mother named him, that means his father was absent. In the Bible, naming sons was the prerogative of fathers. Since his mother had to do it, that means she was all alone and had to assume the responsibilities that should have been shared with his father. Perhaps, what happened is that when Jabez's mother discovered she was pregnant, Jabez's father abandoned her along with their unborn child. Maybe she became bitter every time she looked at Jabez because he reminded her of his father. He had his father's features. When his little brow furrowed, Jabez reminded his mother of the look she once cherished in his father. Instead of dealing with her own feelings of anger and resentment, she decided to curse him with a name that reflected her attitude about his father and what he had done.

One of the challenges for single parents who are dealing with resentment and bitterness after divorce or desertion is not to misdirect their frustrations onto their innocent children. Misdirected bitterness can manifest itself in several ways:

1. Disrespecting the child's need to love and spend time with the other parent.

2. The temptation to use the child as a spy when visiting the other parent.

3. The temptation to use the child as a political pawn to get back at or get back with the other parent.

4. Calling the child names or making disparaging remarks about him/her because you are angry with his/her other parent.

5. Making negative remarks to him or her about their other parent. Criticizing the other parent is the same as criticizing a part of the child.

With such negative baggage and low expectation from his mother, you would think that it would be easy to predict Jabez's future—expelled from school and revolving in and out of the juvenile detention center for car-jacking, gang-banging, and dope peddling.

Praise God that such was not the case for Jabez! Instead of becoming a menace to society, Jabez became a man of honor and respect. He was not a victim of his mother's pronouncements. The text says that Jabez did three things that can be remembered alphabetically.

> *Jabez was more honorable than his brothers. His mother had named him Jabez, saying, "I gave birth to him in pain." Jabez cried out to the God of Israel, "Oh, that you would bless me and enlarge my territory! Let your hand be with me, and keep me from harm so that I will be free from pain." And God granted his request.* (1 Chronicles 4:9-10 NIV)

A—Ambition. Jabez did not allow anyone to steal his ambition. Single parents must do everything to nurture and protect the ambition of their children. The text says that he asked God to bless him. Jabez had a dream. Poverty and racism do not have the power to steal our dreams. There is a law in life called the law of attraction. It simply maintains that we tend to attract things into our lives that reflect our innermost dreams, hopes, beliefs and aspirations. If you are dreaming of or dwelling on small things, you will attract small things. If you are dreaming or dwelling on failure and defeat, that is what you will attract. But if you are dreaming great dreams, you tend to attract greatness.

B—Belief. Nothing is more powerful than the power of belief. Jesus said to the blind men seeking sight, "According to your faith will it be done to you" (Matthew 9:29). Whatever we believe with conviction becomes a part of our reality. The truth of the matter was that Jabez was not sorrowful. He had great potential. But if he had believed that he was sorrowful, even though it was not true, it would have become true in his life. Whatever we believe becomes a part of our reality, even if it is not true.

C—Connect. Jabez connected with a power greater than himself, greater than what his father had done to him by abandoning him, and more powerful than what his mother had done by cursing him with a discouraging name. God's power operating in our lives is always greater than anything that happens to us. The result was that Jabez, the product of a single parent, became more honorable than all his contemporaries.

Ideally, God desires that children be raised in a warm, nurturing, affirming home where they have continuous interaction with a mother and a father. However, if you are a single parent, trying to fill both roles, don't name your child sorrowful! God will direct you to the people and resources that can aid you in bringing out the greatness in your child. Remember not to try and do it alone. The writer of Ecclesiastes is right, "Two are better than one." Still, that does not mean that a single parent family is not a whole unit or that a single parent is not a whole person. What it does mean is that single parents must avail themselves of various support systems that will lift the burden of trying to do it all alone.

— *Musings* —

Answer the following questions on a separate sheet of paper. You may also use these questions to stimulate group discussion.

1. What can single parents do to create a nurturing environment for their children?

2. What resources exist in the church to make single parenting a more wholesome venture?

3. What resources exist in the community and/or church to cause individuals to make a choices regarding having and/or rearing children?

4. What is a dysfunctional family? What are its element? How can one determine when a family is dysfunctional?

5. When God's divine order is violated in the family unit, what are the consequences? How can negative consequences be overcome and changed?

6. Using Bible references, show whether Christians tend to have dysfunctional families or dysfunctional expectations for families?

7. What is the child's responsibility concerning the choices he/she makes?

8. Name some disadvantages of single parenting and explain how there are advantages to having a two-parent family.

9. Review the story of Jabez. What examples for behavior did his father set? What about his mother? How did Jabez respond to his upbringing? What messages and examples did the three of them leave for children today?

10. Think about single parents you know or know of. Name five good examples of single parenting. Cite five examples that could greatly improve their parenting skills.

11. God did indeed design a family unit with a husband and a wife. However, life's circumstances sometimes produces single parents. Since these things happen in life, how can the Church help single parents?

12. How should the Church work to eradicate the bitterness like Jabez's mother felt and other mothers like her feel?

— *Ministries* —

It has been said that whenever you pass a maternity ward, you should bow in respect to the babies. You never know what one of those babies may become. All great men and women start off as babies. When Israel was praying for deliverance from Egyptian captivity, God sent a baby named Moses. Harry Emerson Fosdick described the birth of babies as "the most decisive event in the world." In his book, *Living Under Tension*, Fosdick writes, "If babies are among the main determinants of history, then we never can tell what may happen. Around the corner in a crib may be the tiny hand that will yet push open the door of a new era."

Generally, we think of babies as small and weak, someone for whom we must care. True! But look at history and see how, often, when the world seemed hopeless, when the limits of human achievement seem reached, when the forces arrayed against progress seemed irresistible, a babe was born who became pioneer of a new era.

Single parents should have the same optimistic view of their children that Fosdick addressed in his book. All children are endowed with unlimited potential and possibilities. The goal of good parenting is to guide children to discover that potential and nurture it so that they can grow to become successful adults. A successful adult is a person who is self-reliant, self-disciplined, responsible, and who exercises good judgement in decision-making.

Regardless of how poor or disadvantaged a single parent might be, that parent still has the capacity to develop his/her children into successful adults. For example, if you knew a pregnant woman who already had eight children, three of whom were deaf, two were blind, and one mentally handicapped had syphilis, would you recommend that she have an abortion? If you answered "Yes," then congratulations! You just killed Beethoven.

Wise single parents never limit their children's capacities simply because of the disadvantages or obstacles they may face. Children cannot achieve greatness if greatness is not expected. All parents need to understand the true meaning of greatness. Greatness does not occur when a child is the best. Instead, greatness occurs when a child is his/her best. We are not always able to be the best, but we should always strive to be our best. Success should not be measured by the social image of the child but on his/her character ethic.

In Jesus' parable of the talents (Matthew 25:14-29), Jesus said that each steward was given a different unit of coinage. One was given five, another two, and yet another one. There was no uniformity in the distribution of the coinage, just as there is no uniformity in the distribution of gifts and talents among human beings.

Every child has a least one gift, or perhaps several, which must be carefully and patiently cultivated and nurtured. According to Howard Garner of Harvard University, there are at least ten different forms of intelligence.

1. **Verbal Intelligence** — the ability to speak and having command of one's language.

2. **Mathematical Intelligence** — the ability to work with numbers.

3. **Physical Intelligence** — athletic timing, agility and coordination of the body.

4. **Musical Intelligence** — the ability create and make music.

5. **Visual-spatial Intelligence** — the ability to draw pictures, produce art, design buildings.

6. **Interpersonal Intelligence** — the ability to communicate, negotiate and influence other people.

7. **Intrapersonal Intelligence** — Knowing yourself, knowing who you are, knowing what you want out of life, and knowing how to set goals and develop strategies and plans to reach personal goals.

8. **Entrepreneurial Intelligence** — the ability to establish businesses, and to market and to sell a product that meets consumer needs.

9. **Intuitive Intelligence** — the ability to determine whether a situation is right or wrong.

10. **Abstract Intelligence** — the ability to think in the abstract, as did Albert Einstein.

All children are born with some form of intelligence. The question for all parents is whether that intelligence be discovered, cultivated and nurtured? The Church can assist single parents in this important task.

SPARK

Every church needs to establish a SPARK fellowship for single parents. SPARK is an acronym for Single Parents Activating Resourceful Kids. One of the obstacles that might have to be overcome in starting a SPARK fellowship in a local church is dispelling the myth that support groups are for people with problems and dysfunctionalities. In fact, the opposite is true. Serious problems are more likely to arise among people who have no access to support groups.

Remember what is written in the Book of Ecclesiastes: "Two are better than one ... woe be unto the person who is alone." This principle can be applied to everything from block watch clubs to clergy support groups.

A support group is formed when two or more people engage in dialogue about mutual concerns and collaborate to achieve some mutually desirable objective. The church of the 21st Century must provide a plethora of support groups that are relevant and needs-responsive. For example, at St. Stephen Church, we have support groups for ministers, men, women, married couples, cancer patients, singles, unemployed persons, cocaine addicts, alcoholics, and SPARK.

A SPARK fellowship should endeavor to do the following:

1. Elect officers who will provide leadership and direction.

2. Host a monthly meeting that is announced to the church body and community at large. Professionals should be invited to these meetings to address topics of importance to single parents. As SPARK continues to grow, the group may need to be divided into smaller cell groups.

3. Develop and maintain Big Brother/Big Sister-type programs that enable kids to have a multiplicity of role models.

4. Develop and maintain a single parents' resource bank that details all of the resources and services available to assist single parents.

5. Work with the youth ministry and Sunday School to develop a Parents' Night Out. This should be conducted at least four times annually. This ministry event will give single parents an opportunity to leave their children at a supervised church function so that they can have personal time.

6. Publish and maintain a monthly or quarterly SPARK newsletter containing information and articles of importance to single parents.

7. Sponsor an annual single parents' conference that addresses the concerns of single parents.

8. Have all children study and sign the GREAT covenant card. GREAT is an acronym for:

   • Get connected to God and Church!

   • Remain in school and get a good education.

   • Eliminate all behavior that will get you in trouble with the police and the judicial system.

   • Accept an honorable, entry level job in order to become acclimated to the world of work.

   • Teenage pregnancy is eliminated only through abstinence.

— BIBLIOGRAPHY —

Artrurburn, Stephen and Jack Felton. *Toxic Faith.* Nashville: Thomas Nelson Publishers, 1991.

Baldwin, James. *The Fire Next Time.* New York: Vintage Books, 1993.

Barboza, Steven. *The African American Book of Values: Classic Moral Stories.* New York: Doubleday, 1998.

Barclay, Mark. *The Real Truth About Tithing.* M. Barclay Publications,1994.

Bennett, William J. ed. *The Moral Compass: Stories for a Life's Journey.* Touchstone Books, 1992.

> *The Book of Virtues: A Treasury of Great Moral Stories.* New York: Simon and Schuster, 1993.

Berry, Carmen Renee. *When Helping You Is Hurting Me: Escaping the Messiah Trap.* New York: HarperCollins, 1988.

Burkett, Larry. *How to Manage Your Money.* Chicago: Moody Press, 1991.

Clarke, Dr. John Henrik. *Black Family Conferences.* Louisville: University of Louisville, 1994.

Cloud, Olivia M., compiler. *Black Baptist Sunday School Growth.* Nashville: Convention Press, 1990.

Dubois, W.E.B. *The Souls of Black Folk.* New York: Signet Classics/Nal Penguin, Inc., 1903.

Ellison, Ralph. *Invisible Man.* New York: Vintage Books, 1995.

Fields, Doug. *Would You Rather?* Grand Rapids: Zondervan Publishing House, 1996.

Fosdick, Harry Emerson. *Living Under Tension: Sermons on Christianity Today.* New: York: Harper & Brothers, 1941.

Hansel, Tim. *When I Relax, I Feel Guilty.* Colorado Springs: Chariot Victor, 1979.

Kelsey, George. *Racism and the Christian Understanding of Man.* New York: Charles Scribners' Sons, 1965.

Lynch, Peter, and Rohn Rothchild. *Learn to Earn: A Beginner's Guide to the Basics of Investing and Business.* New York: Fireside,1996.

McKnight, John. *The Careless Society.* New York,:Basic Books, 1996.

Perkins, John M. *Restoring At-Risk Communities.* Grand Rapids, MI: Baker Books, 1995.

Pinson, William. *The Local Church in Ministry.* Nashville: Broadman Press, 1973.

Roberts, Deotis J. *Black Theology and Dialogue.* Philadelphia: Westminster Press, 1987.

Russell, Bob. *Take Comfort.* Cincinnati: The Standard Publishing Company, 1991.

Stanley, Charles. *Understanding Financial Stewardship.* Nashville: Thomas Nelson, 1997.

Steele, Shelby. *The Content of Our Character.* New York: Harperperennial Library, 1991.

Stoop, David and Stephen Arterburn. *Life Recovery Bible.* Carol Stream: Tyndale House Publishers, 1992.

Waters, Ethel. *To Me, It's Wonderful.* New York: Harper & Row, 1972.

Woodson, Carter G. *The Miseducation of the Negro.* New York: AMS Press, 1973.

Wright, Jeremiah, compiler. *No Other Help I Know: Sermons on Prayer and Spirituality.* Valley Forge: Judson Press, 1996.

— ABOUT THE AUTHOR —

Kevin W. Cosby, D.Min.

A staunch proponent of education, Dr. Cosby earned a Bachelor's degree from Eastern Kentucky University in Richmond, a Master of Divinity degree from The Southern Baptist Theological Seminary in Louisville, and a Doctor of Ministry degree from United Theological Seminary in Dayton, Ohio. He has been awarded honorary doctorates from Eastern Kentucky University, Bellarmine University, and Campbellsville University.

Dr. Cosby has held administrative and teaching assignments at Kentucky State University, the University of Louisville, The Southern Baptist Theological Seminary, and United Theological Seminary. His exceptional oratory skills have produced lecture engagements at universities and institutions around the world, including Harvard University. His local community service includes boards of trustees for both Kentucky State University and the University of Louisville.

ST. STEPHEN BAPTIST CHURCH

Since 1979, the Reverend Dr. Kevin W. Cosby has served as Senior Pastor of St. Stephen Baptist Church in Louisville, Kentucky. Due greatly to his practical and dynamic Bible teachings, the congregation has grown from 500 to approximately 14,000 members with three large beautifully appointed campuses: a 1,000-seat church in Louisville, and 500-seat churches in Jeffersonville, Indiana and Radcliff, Kentucky. The church conducts mid-week Bible studies and multiple services on Saturdays and Sundays to accommodate the crowds. It also broadcasts its full worship services weekly at www.ssclive.tv.

In 2010 *Outreach* magazine recognized St. Stephen as one of the 100 largest churches in America, and *Emerge* magazine identified it as one of six "super churches" of the South. St. Stephen has the largest Christian African American education program in Kentucky and sponsors development of the full person, through education, science, art, music, and culture. Annually it awards $50,000 in college scholarships.

Under Dr. Cosby's vision, St. Stephen has grown to become the largest private black employer in Kentucky and has led the city's economic investment in one of the poorest neighborhoods in the nation. Dr. Cosby's leadership brings blacks and whites together to channel social and economic capital into poor neighborhoods. Dr. Cosby promotes black entrepreneurship, hard work, self-reliance, accountability, and ethical wealth building. St. Stephen leads by example. A debt-free institution controlled by blacks, its $23 million in assets include more contiguous property than any other black private institution in West Louisville.

St. Stephen is dedicated to service and to justice. It speaks up for the poor, promotes voter registration drives, conducts health clinics, and provides transportation for seniors. At no cost to the city, it renovated the nearby California Community Center, and It established and built a Family Life Center, which includes a state-of-the-art indoor fitness center, racquet ball court, basketball court, an indoor walking/running track, an upscale women's clothing boutique, a sit-down family restaurant, youth after school and summer enrichment programs, and addiction recovery meetings. It also has provided facilities for West Louisville's only physical therapy rehabilitation center. More information on this visionary church is found at www.ssclive.org.

SIMMONS COLLEGE OF KENTUCKY INC.

While St. Stephen Baptist Church is Dr. Cosby's first calling, Simmons College of Kentucky Inc. has become his mission outreach project. From 1879 to 1930, Simmons College was a national leader in higher education for African Americans. Established by formerly enslaved Kentucky Baptists, Simmons became a full university with a law school and a medical school. But during the Great Depression, its campuses suffered foreclosure, and as its programs were scaled back, it became a small Bible college in a remote part of the city's poorest area.

In 1997, Dr. Cosby led his church to purchase the nearby four-acres of the former Simmons campus, even though at the time, he was unsure of how the property would be used. He prayed in his heart that God would allow him to reclaim the mission of this historically black institution of higher learning, even though, at the time, it seemed like a pipe dream. Yet in 2005 Dr. Kevin Cosby became the 13th president of Simmons and promptly began reclaiming the college's original mission of offering a full curriculum for impoverished African American youth.

In the last 12 years, Dr. Cosby has refused nearly $1,000,000 in compensation that would otherwise be due to someone of his stature in order to assure the college's economic stability and build a comprehensive curriculum. Simmons' priority is students, maintaining a small faculty-student ratio, and it embraces entrepreneurial education. Under Dr. Cosby's visionary leadership, Simmons gained accreditation by the Association of Biblical Higher Education (ABHE). In 2015 the U.S. Department of Education granted Simmons status as the nation's 107th Historically Black College and University (HBCU). Enrolling over 200 students, Simmons offers baccalaureate and associate degrees in business, cross-cultural communications, music, religious studies, and sociology—all designed to strengthen the five institutions so critical to the African American community: churches, families, schools, businesses, and media. In the last two years, Simmons has graduated 55 students, all of whom have completed college with zero debt.

Simmons has recently become the headquarters for the National Baptist Convention of America International Inc. (NBCA). An organization first formed in1880, this voluntary convention of African American Baptists has over 3.5 million constituents. This will be a beneficial relationship for the college, the convention, and the city. The NBCA has already purchased a beautiful 56-acre retreat/conference center in southwestern Louisville, and its annual sessions will bring attention to Simmons and tourism to the city, while Simmons' program in religious studies and its community leadership programs will support the mission of the convention.

Simmons College and the NBCA along with the Progressive Baptist Convention Inc., and the Cooperative Baptist Fellowship have partnered together to sponsor a three-year comprehensive religious and community education program that creates awareness of our individual and collective responsibility to do God's work of economic justice—leading up to the 400th anniversary of slavery in America. Known as the Angela Project in honor of the first Christian enslaved woman to step foot on American soil in 1619, the program will bring leaders together to advocate for black communities and institutions in places of power, challenge businesses and churches to invest in black neighborhoods, while teaching black communities to better use their economic resources.

PUBLICATIONS

Dr. Cosby has authored five highly-acclaimed books: *Get off Your But!: Messages, Musings & Ministries to Empower the African-American Church*; *As They Went*; *Treasure Worth Seeking*; *Who's Your Daddy?: Life Lessons from the Prodigal Son* and *Be Loyal to the Royal*. He has been a contributing writer to a number of books, journals, and newspapers.

PERSONAL AND CONTACT INFORMATION

Dr. Kevin Cosby has been the subject of many national articles and documentaries, which consistently list him among the most influential leaders in the Commonwealth of Kentucky. His 2007 selection as "Louisvillian of the Year" is a tribute to his outstanding contributions to the community. *Louisville Magazine* ranked him #1 of the Top Ten Religious Leaders in Louisville. In the spring of 2012, he was inducted into the Hall of Distinguished Alumni at Eastern Kentucky University. Although Dr. Cosby has achieved many notable accomplishments, he is most known for his intense commitment to serving God through improving the lives of others.

Dr. Cosby is married to the former Barnetta Turner. They are the parents of two adult children and one beautiful grand-daughter.

To contact Dr. Cosby for more information regarding his ministries and community leadership activities or for speaking engagements, email seniorpastor@ssclive.org or phone: 502-583-6798. More information may be found at http://www.drkevincosby.com.

— OTHER BOOKS —

by Kevin W. Cosby, D. min.

AS THEY WENT...
Dr. Cosby examines the testimonies of God's faithful followers who experienced His blessings, mercy, and grace because they chose the route of obedience to God. In his sermons and writings, Dr. Cosby presents well-known Bible stories in a fresh way. After reading this book, you will understand Enoch, Abraham, Moses, Peter, Philip, and others in a new way that is relevant to your own life. This book is not the same old clichés about obeying worn-out platitudes, but about empowering people as they answer the call of God.

BE LOYAL TO THE ROYAL IN YOU
Previously published as *Treasure Worth Seeking*, Dr. Cosby examines five ways that believers benefit from being a royal priesthood—in wisdom, truth, guidance, power, and joy. Being a royal is not just an abstract pious status you attain, but an understanding your divine heritage that enables you to attain excellence in all areas of your life

GET OFF YOUR BUT!
In this new paradigm for the proclamation of the Gospel, Dr. Cosby examines twelve challenges that face all communities. He not only gives inspiring biblical examples of meeting those challenges, but also outlines practical ways that churches can make a difference in the lives of those they serve. While set in the context of the African American church, this book speaks to all churches that want to show the love of Christ to people in a real way. When you read this book, your life will be better, your community will be stronger, and your church will be more relevant. But first, you must get off your but!

JESUS GREW, SO HOW ABOUT YOU?

This book looks at Jesus' life, both the recorded and hidden parts, to glean important lessons about personal growth. Christians say they want to be like Jesus, but they overlook the clues in Scripture about how growth truly occurs. The majority of Jesus' life and preparation went unrecorded, hidden from our eyes. Growth toward maturity takes much time, humility, and discipline and is unseen by others before we can make a public show. Centered on Luke 2:52, Dr. Cosby shows readers how personal growth must include all areas of our lives: physical, educational, spiritual, and social.

WHO'S YOUR DADDY?

Using vivid imagery and true-to-life situations, Dr. Cosby offers hope that every person can be united with their heavenly Father in a healthy relationship. Dr. Cosby explores how the Prodigal Son's experience mirrors the life cycle of every individual's relationship with God. Within the context of the African American male, Dr. Cosby shows how cultivating a relationship with God can heal the wounds of our absent or imperfect fathers and can enable us to have better relationships in all areas of our lives. Reading this book will forever transform the way you view the story of the prodigal son.

Most titles available at the St. Stephen Baptist Church bookstore, Simmons College of Kentucky bookstore, other Christian bookstores ,and Amazon.com. E-book editions available at www.drkevincosby.com,

www.ingramcontent.com/pod-product-compliance
Lightning Source LLC
LaVergne TN
LVHW051256080426
835509LV00020B/3008